G000160624

Acknowledgements:

Tricia Kirby: for thoroughly and painstakingly
proof-reading

Spruce Lynch: for being the driver, travelling companion
and initial proof reader

Ruth Queally: for initial map designs

Contents

Introduction

The aim of these trails is to help people find places that often are not signposted. There is an emphasis in this book on early Christian and more ancient archaeological sites, since the Burren is ripe with such sites. I also refer to some hostelries and other current places of human interest as this guide is for the general visitor to the region. There are some references to ley lines and earth energies as some visitors will be drawn to this area due to the intense energy and rarity of the Burren landscape.

There are plenty of books on the rare botany of the Burren so I do not include much information on the natural science of the Burren. I would recommend visitors to be mindful of the plants and animals as they walk about and to appreciate each site as a haven of peace in this busy world we live in.

For each itinerary there is an audio version available to download at

http://www.earthwise.me/product/burren-trails-audio/

This is intended for cyclists, bikers and drivers who would benefit from listening as they drive.

Of course this book can also be read as a stand alone guide so you can get a taste of what the Burren has to offer before travelling there yourself!

I hope you all enjoy this work of labour and love.

Jackie Queally January 2015

www.earthwise.me

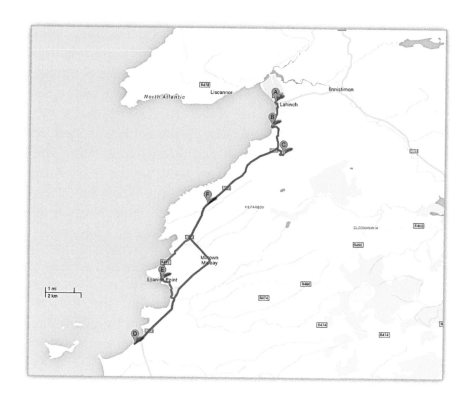

LAHINCH TRAIL 1

TOTAL DISTANCE ☞ 40.1 km

AUDIO FILE:

http://www.earthwise.me/product/burren-trails-audio/

POINT A: LAHINCH N 52.93212° W009.04528° (henceforth all co-ordinates will be written in the style 52.93212, -009.04528)

Meaning "half island", this once minute fishing village first blossomed into a golfing centre in 1907 and more recently has burgeoned into a very popular surfing centre.

The O'Connors, the medieval chieftains in this area, held Dough Castle that is long gone. The successor landlords, the O'Briens, took over the site in 1584 and their castle remains, overlooking the seventh hole of the golf course – lucky for some.. Only one tower remains of this small complex. Dough Castle was known in Irish as O'Connor's Sandbank and its very sandy foundations led to creating an iconic ruin. The adjacent sand hills are the legendary haunt of the Fairy King and prince of the Tuatha de Danaan, Donn of the Sandhills. A significant local festival called Garland Sunday was held in Lahinch until recent times. It has its roots in a pagan festival in honour of this fairy king.

Another haunted sandhill was Crughaneer near the bridge you cross on the way to Liscannor. My grandmother used to tell me tales of the Sidhe or fairies as she sat by her range on their coastal farm here, and it is in memory of this softly spoken lady that I dedicate this audio book. Like so many of her neighbours long deceased, she had a true sense of community spirit that is rare to find in this modern world.

This area of Clare is widely known for its musicians, such as Willy Clancy who lived from 1918 until his early demise in 1973. Willy was most renowned as a piper but he was talented on many other instruments, including his own voice! A summer school and festival in his honour continues to this day in his hometown of Miltown Malbay. For the first part of our journey together let's take the coast road towards Milltown Malbay.

RESUME WHEN READY

Leave Lahinch heading south on the coast road N67 towards Kilrush. About half a mile south of Lahinch is a small bay called Craig which is overlooked by an unusual house with a square tower. You may park on the far side of the bend here. Be careful as you cross the road at the bend to park in the small parking area under the metal gateway.

POINT B: MOY HOUSE 52.917339, -9.349154   1.4 km

MOY HOUSE

This is now a small hotel set in the townland of Moy, which means "a plain". 'Moy" is a very common place name in Irish. Moy House stands on the remaining fragment of a large estate that once belonged to the Fitzgeralds, a family described as being "more Irish than the Irish" since their ancestors acquired and supported Gaelic customs and ideologies. My family come from this townland and they imparted a sense of egalitarianism on me from a young age.

RESUME WHEN READY

Continue on the coast road south – soon it bends sharp right and goes through a railway cutting just before the turning for Moy House. Turn left at the next junction and drive to the top of the hill where there is a small housing scheme on the left hand side. Park on the left hand lay-by before the entrance to the small housing estate.

Once the West Clare railway ran through this land, and I remember my uncle hailing the train to stop on our farm. They have revived a small section of the steam train journey at Moyasta Station between Kilkee and Kilrush, further down the Clare coastline. Cross over the road and visit a community garden enterprise that shares a seasonal produce table each Friday.

POINT C:
MOY HILL COMMUNITY GARDEN 52.883634, -9.397602   3.7 km

This initiative was set up by a bunch of surfers who found they had spare time on their hands. The scheme is taking hold and various local fields are being added to the scheme. The foraging pigs and the vegetables are mainly grown in a field by Moy House, mentioned just beforehand.

RESUME WHEN READY

Return to the bottom of the hill and turn left to continue along the coast road. After six km you enter the area known as Rineen, where you can stop later to view an (old) IRA war memorial on the way back to Lahinch. For now just continue along the coast road, and after 8.8 km you reach Milltown Malbay, where you turn right along the main street and continue through for Quilty. Soon you come to the small fishing village of Quilty, that still looks similar to how I remember it as a child fifty years ago. As the main N67 road veers left away from the sea wall take the turning to the right instead, which is almost straight ahead, heading out towards the headland. You should shortly see a small church with a round tower on the left hand side. Pull into the large car park on the right by the seafront.

STAR OF THE SEA CHURCH

This is the Star of the Sea, a church built with money partly donated from French citizens, who wanted to show their gratitude to the fishermen of Quilty for saving the lives of 13 French sailors shipwrecked from their stricken freight ship in a storm in October 1907. Sadly 9 Frenchmen perished in the storm. This is a beautiful church in the Hiberno-Romanesque style. Its distinct round tower is similar to one I know of at an old site called Arraid, on the Isle of Mull. The tower here is a symbolic landmark for sailors. There has been some refurbishment to this church. Nowadays the church is a veritable haven with calming background music and several beautifully adorned altars. It has several interesting windows with Biblical references to the sea. It is well worth spending some time here. Since 1949 the bell from the shipwrecked Leon is on display in the vestibule, adding poignancy to this tale. Look out to sea here and ponder the name "Quilty" which stems from *Coilte* that is Irish for woods. There were extensive hazel woods here long ago. The woods were destroyed when in 804 AD an earthquake along the coast killed over 1000 people, and resulted in creating Mutton Island offshore. In places tree stumps are still discovered on the sandy shores.

The Spanish in the late sixteenth century did not seem to fare as well as the French seamen. Several boats of the Spanish Armada were wrecked along these coasts, and any known survivors were not spared by the English rulers, who were unaware that the Spanish had been already defeated by the English fleet elsewhere. Spanish Point nearby gets its name from this murky chapter in Clare history.

One ship ran aground off Mutton Island and lost around 450 men when it sank! It was in fact a Portuguese galleon. Interestingly it sank on the Autumn Equinox as did the French freight in a later century. Some locals (including my grandfather when he was alive) swear that some Spaniards survived, settled and even procreated–accounting for the dark looks of number of the locals along the western seaboard here.

If you wish to continue on the coast road towards Kilkee you can pass through this seaside hamlet and reach Kilrush. In summer there is a ferry from the harbour area that takes you to Scattery Island, an ancient Christian settlement. There you can find remains of many medieval churches that were more than likely built over earlier Celtic ones. There is a legendary holy well and a partly ruined Irish round tower there also. This was the sanctuary of St Senan, a renowned Celtic saint in the region. He is said to have destroyed a dragon that lurks in Doo Lough, about ten kilometres inland from Quilty on back roads.

RESUME WHEN READY

Now retrace your steps toward Lahinch passing again through Milltown Malbay and taking a left hand turn at the far end of the main street to drive along the coast road. Take the R482 signposted to your left to visit Spanish POINT. This road is on the corner with the Bellbridge Hotel, a pleasant, modest hotel on your left.

STOP E: SPANISH POINT 52.905589, -9.344559   4.7 km

Why not take lunch at the Armada Hotel at Spanish Point where you can enjoy splendid vistas of the dramatic Atlantic coastline?

RESUME WHEN READY

Afterwards, carry straight on along the headland. The road returns you to the main N67 where you turn left for Lahinch.

The next stop is an unusual one already mentioned. It is a war memorial dedicated to the successful efforts success of local soldiers of the 'old' IRA. *When you pass a turning for Feach Church on the left slow down as the road bends to the left below some gorse cliffs on the right hand side. The monument is carved in a recess in the cliffs and you can park in a small gap just before a boreen (track) on the left.*

RINEEN MONUMENT

This monument commemorates a rare, successful IRA ambush at Rineen on around the Autumn Equinox in 1920. My grandfather took part as a lieutenant in the 4th Battalion Mid Clare Brigade of the old IRA. These were the days when Ireland was fighting for independence from Britain. She was occupied by the often cruel forces of the British Army, in addition to mercenary or irregular soldiers known as the Black and Tans. Unfortunately, this local Irish success met with severe and swift reprisals in the surrounding countryside and villages. There was a heavy price paid for the creation of the "Free State" of Ireland, including the bloody civil war that followed in its wake.

RESUME WHEN READY

Continue on the beautiful coast road as far as the seaside town of Lahinch where you started.

Lahinch   52.93212, -009.04528   8.1 km

End of Lahinch Trail 1

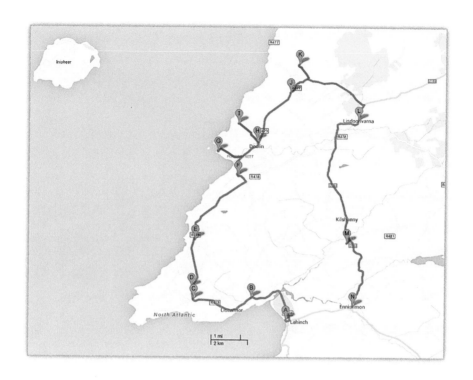

LAHINCH TRAIL 2

TOTAL DISTANCE ☞ 53.1 km

AUDIO FILE:

http://www.earthwise.me/product/burren-trails-audio/

POINT A: LAHINCH 52.93212, -009.04528

LAHINCH PROMENADE

I can remember in the 60s entering a small shop in Lahinch, now occupied by the well established Celtic T Shirt Shop. In those days it seemed to me to be an almost empty premises, filled to capacity however by the benign presences of the elderly couple who owned it. They had a freezer which opened up to display a few ice cream varieties–and my favourite one was their vanilla ice cream block, which they would take out for me. Then they would hover over it with a large cutting knife, asking how much I had to spend. After I had showed them my penny they would swipe the knife half way across the block and ask me if that was enough for me! I would tell them it was too much and then they would playfully move the knife back and forth across the block until I cried "Stop". This banter had a great effect on me as a child and I would inwardly compare the exchange to where I lived in London's West End, where your money was matched exactly to the monetary value of the product. I loved this apparent elasticity of time and generosity of being in Lahinch, and the whole of the west of Ireland to that matter. I appreciated the way the local folk seemed to wear their heart on their sleeves!

I later learnt that the folk in this part of Ireland were renowned for their generosity of spirit and their strong emotional connection to the land. Their traditional songs and dances echoed these sentiments. A more ancient earth-bound consciousness dwelt in these people until the motor car and TV era swept it away only 40 years ago.

RESUME WHEN READY

In Lahinch take the coast road R478 west past the golf course, world-renowned for its challenging course.

Before Irish Independence the O'Briens were the ruling family in the area, and the small bridge that straddles the joined rivers of the Daelagh and Inagh is still known as "O' Brien's Bridge". When the tide is out you can walk the spit of land leading up to it from the golf course and view the flatfish that swim in the deep channel. There are dangerous quicksands in the river delta so do not stray far.

Continue for about two kilometres until you see a signpost to the left for MacCreehy's old church by the sand dunes. It is after a brown tourist sign for the Cliffs of Moher. Drive down and park in the small car park.

POINT B: ST MCCREEHY'S CHURCH   52.943584, -9.375958   3.5 km

RUINS OF ST MACREEHY CHURCH

St Macreehy lived in the sixth century and is associated with mythical dragons and eels! He is said to have chased a corpse-eating eel into Liscannor Bay–there used to be a stone carving here referencing this legend. It suffered the same fate as the eel in that it vanished into the night. One of the lintels in the ruin shows a remnant of a dragon or eel with a human bone in its jaw if you look hard! I see the beast more as a cat with pointed ears. Wherever myths reside of early saints slaying dragons/eels/serpents it denotes that the local site emits strong, yet subtle, energies that rendered it sacred in past times when folk were more connected to the land. The early saints without a doubt sensed such energies. St Macreehy's Church is one of the earliest Christian sites in County Clare. Early Christians mixed pagan customs with their new religion. Certainly archaeologists and folklorists feel that Macreehy's site might have been a pagan site of worship too. According to Westropp, an intrepid folklorist from over one hundred years ago, there was a fine beast depicted on Mac-Creehy's grave. Once when I visited the church I met some local men who confirmed that it had been removed. It would have been rather unusual to have a decorative gravestone in the seventh century—the stone would have lain flat in the ground. Macreehy is said to have his "bed" on the sands below the church. He might well have been buried in the sand. The present church was built in the 15th century and there is nothing of the early one left. In my book Spirit of the Burren I examine Macreehy's life in more depth.

Another legend that might have some normal reality to it that of Kilstephen or Kilstapheen, a buried church and associated village beneath the waters in Liscannor Bay. At the turn of the ninth century, a huge tidal wave caused by an earthquake killed between one and two thousand folk who dwelt along the coastline here. The submerged city of Kilstephen has been described as an enchanted golden city with domes upon its roof. The key to unlock the gates to the city lie under the warrior Conan's mythical tomb. Deep-sea divers have explored great dives, through arches and over ridges and mounds out in the bay. They tell me that there are bogs and forests on a shelf out to sea indicating a substantial loss of land. In addition, tree stumps are found all along the beaches of this part of Clare. When the earthquake arose it split some of the coast into three islands from just south of here as far as the mouth of the Shannon. Mutton Island just south of Lahinch was one of these islands. In these unsettling climatic times the coast may change rapidly again.

Interestingly a submarine beast of another kind is associated with Liscannor too. The inventor of the prototype for the mass-produced submarine was born in Liscannor in1840.

John P. Holland emigrated to the US where the Holland sub-marine was launched in 1897.

RESUME WHEN READY.

Continue on the R487 into Liscannor and follow the road on towards the famous Cliffs of Moher, and as the road climbs and bends right, it reaches a plateau with a large shop and car park on the right where you can pull in.

POINT C: THE ROCK SHOP   52.946052, -9.424408   3.6 km

The Rock Shop is strategically placed on a hill overlooking the bay. Owned by the local Johnson family who also own the large tourist attraction Ailwee Cave, it is a fascinating enterprise, chronicling the history of the limestone quarrying industry in Liscannor. Liscannor flagstones are used in diverse ways in the building industry to this day. The main part of this shop is dedicated to selling gemstones and arte-facts to the tourists and its pleasant cafe offers a stunning view over the bay. You get an almost aerial view of Liscannor Bay from here, and perhaps you can sense the dragon lurking in its waters, waiting to re-emerge.

RESUME WHEN READY

Continue up the hill a short distance and then turn left opposite a large memorial pillar. Park opposite on the right outside the side entrance to the holy well here. The pillar was built in honour of the local landlord Cornelius O'Brien, who was by all written accounts a sympathetic landlord and politician. He advocated developing tourism by promoting the natural beauty of the surrounds, and the visionary's memorial is fittingly sited only a short distance away from Ireland's major tourist attraction these days: the Cliffs of Moher.

ST BRIGID'S WELL

In the quiet lee of the massive column lies St Brigid's Well, one of Ireland's most revered holy wells. Before entering the long passage, consider the juxtaposition of tall column and well. From around 1840 the Roman Catholic Church ordered the steady and quiet removal of many phallic like natural stones that were placed beside holy wells. This, in effect, robbed the place of its role and higher purpose. The indigenous culture had honoured the role nature played in their lives, and the "Pillar" and womb-like well were known to represent and embody two vital aspects of the whole. By removing the old symbol of masculinity, the feminine energy was robbed of her sense of balance and power. Like many other places, when Ireland became disconnected from its native culture, a new culture of religion gained an unnatural and imbalanced domination only recently being acknowledged in Irish society. It only took a little time for Ireland to lose its language too, but holy wells remain as one of the few symbols of Ireland's past wisdom and deep connection to the divine in nature that many indigenous cultures respect.

St Brigit's well passage is heavily adorned with religious relics. By walking the path up to the cemetery you can look down over the wellhead—and walking further up you can stand above the water as it cascades down from the source. These manmade waterfalls can be viewed from near the roadside further along.

Ley lines are like subtle energy lines that emanate from the earth. According to an English researcher Tony Peart there is a strong ley line streaming inland from the cliffs that passes through the holy well here. Leys often pass through wells, providing a boost to the subtle energies of any electro-magnetic field. This combination of ley activity and pure spring water make such places special and holy.

RESUME WHEN READY

Continue on the road and a large green hill camouflaging an extensive visitor centre will loom into view on the left. Soon you will come to the official car park for the Cliffs of Moher on the right hand side where you can park.

POINT E: CLIFFS OF MOHER CENTRE 52.973041, -9.423444   2.4 km

This is where my grandfather would accompany us on home visits. There used to be a small ice cream kiosk in O'Brien's Tower on the cliffs, in the days when there were no defensive walls around the cliffs! On most days, even in summer, we might be the only visitors walking the cliffs. As they say, how times have changed! With the increase in international travel, visitors can enjoy both a marvellous cliff walk and an architectural experience, as the visitor centre is built into the hillside here. A geological film of the unique Burren is well presented here. There is also a relatively new longer distance cliff top walk you can start in either Liscannor or Doolin.

RESUME WHEN READY

After experiencing the majesty of the Cliffs of Moher, travel on the road towards Doolin which is only a few miles away – take the steep road left at the first crossroads you come to and pull in on the right to view the fairytale castle of Doonagore, the unfortunate site of hanging of several shipwrecked prisoners from the Spanish Armada. (If you turn too soon you'll pass Clare Jams, so then turn right at the T junction and head toward Doolin and the castle will appear on the right–you can stop by the cattle grid before the next T junction to take photos of this enchanting castle. You would then turn left at the junction to continue to Doolin.

DOONAGORE CASTLE

Now owned privately by an American family, the castle features in my book Spirit of the Burren, since it is at the tip of the larger arm of an elongated pentagram discovered by Tony Peart, the English geometer who discovered the earth grid over the Burren. The main ley line from here travels to a sacred mountain in East Norway, where coincidentally another friend and researcher also discovered a similar pentagram, albeit on a much larger scale! The process of discovering the pentagram that spans the whole of southern Norway is described in Harald Boehlke's book, The Norwegian Pentagram, which is stocked in all libraries in Norway. It was translated into English as the Viking Serpent. The author of this intriguing research maintains that it was Irish monks leaving the west of Ireland who sailed to Norway and commandeered the construction of Norway's first Christian cathedrals, many of which were in unlikely places. The siting of Norway's first cathedral cities created a geometric pentagram when measured over long distances. Could it have been Norway where, in the Irish medieval saga, or imram, *The Maeldun,* the monks found distant shores of abundant resources? Could the monks have set off from Doolin? It is quite likely, for in the Middle Ages, sailors often intuited ley lines at sea that guided them along unknown routes, much in the way aboriginal cultures use leys to walk long distances on the land.

RESUME WHEN READY

Continue towards Doolin on the coast by turning right at the T junction below the castle (or continuing straight if on the small coast road that passed Clare Jams earlier). Where the road swings to the right you could park and join the public walk along the cliffs of Moher to the left. Otherwise, continue onto Doolin and take the small road to the left over the bridge at the bottom of the hill. Go down Fisher St past the tiny gift shops to the pier, and park in the car park on the right–there are toilets at the far end in case you need them.

POINT G: DOOLIN PIER 53.014886, -9.404415   2.7 km

From the pier you can hop on a ferry to the Aran Isles, where many an early monk lived in contemplative exile. You can even take a ferry along the base of the 700 feet cliffs to experience them from a different angle, and spot freshwater springs issuing forth from the base of the cliffs if you are lucky enough. Don't forget to visit a pub or two in Doolin for some good food, music and "craic" (witty or lively conversation).

RESUME WHEN READY

Continue north along the coast road out of Doolin and soon you will be in Roadford, signposted on the left. When you cross a small river there is a pub called McDermotts on the right hand side and a cycle rack opposite on the left hand side. Take the small road to the left which has many tourist signs on it, including one to Roadford House Restaurant. This road takes you past Killilagh Church on the right.

POINT H: KILLILAGH CHURCH 53.004145, -9.388174   2.9 km

This church has some graceful ogee windows and an interesting adjacent mausoleum. This empty Macnamara tomb was once used as a jail! Like Rathbourney, one of my favourite churches in the Burren, this church appears to have been built over a tumulus or burial ground.

RESUME WHEN READY

Drive on to the end of the lane and stop.

POINT I: COURT CHAMBER 53.028671, -9.387309 (end of road)
1.6 km

Among this commonage and scrub there are many ring forts, one with an underground souterrain or larder, and large landmark rocks once known by their Irish names. These are in fact glacial deposits of granite from across the bay in Connemara. Close to here are the ruins of one of the chief types of ancient Irish burial; a court chamber.

To reach it, climb over the wall at the low stile and follow the path in the direction of the sea and slightly to the right.

Court chambers have both inner and outer chambers, the latter acting more like a courtyard – whereas wedge shaped tombs are single chambers with roofs, and dolmens have two end stones and a large overhanging roof stone so it resembles a table on legs. There are more dolmens in the Burren than in any other part of Ireland.

This court tomb has a presence even in its ruined state among the brambles. I remember this site was more intact thirty years ago.

RESUME WHEN READY

Return to the main road and if you want to visit a local cave with a massive stalactite, stop near the junction and visit the 'Bruach na Aille Restaurant' beside the pub on the right to purchase tickets. Continue north along the coast road. After seven minutes or so driving you come to the cave 'Pol an Ionain' which is well worth a visit. You will see a black sign for it on the left and the opening is on the right. There is a nice nature walk here too.

POINT J: POL AN IONAIN 53.045032, -9.344757   4.9 km

The whole of the Burren has a network of underground rivers that have formed dry and wet passages and caves which potholers and cavers can explore with the right equipment. It was cavers who discovered this 23 feet long stalactite in 1952. Professor David Drew is one of Ireland's foremost speleologists. Now retired from Trinity College I had the good fortune to accompany him once down an underground cave containing a rushing waterfall within a narrow cavern. I shall never forget twisting around awkward protruding rocks and then hearing the rush of underground water. How utterly refreshing it was to perch beside this subterranean waterfall! There is far more river activity underground than overground in the Burren. Water finds its way through the fissures and cracks in the limestone, for the softness of the rock allows water to enter with ease. I believe it is the presence of vast underground stores of water that can engender a strong emotional response to this landscape, for science has shown that water subtly alters 'the earth's electro-magnetic frequencies which in turn affects humans in subtle, beneficial ways.

RESUME WHEN READY

A little further up the road there is a staggered junction. You are now facing the entrance to Ballynalacken Castle, a fine country home with good dining. *Turn left at the junction and almost immediately fork right uphill along a road* that takes you into a wild and rocky part of the Burren, with scenic cliffs in the distance. *Soon there is a road to the right to Lisdoonvarna. Just past this, there is a road on the left that goes between two houses. One is a cream coloured pebbledash bungalow. Go down the road into a sheltered hollow. Before the delightful cottage at the very end of the road, there is a clearing on the right on a bend where you can park. Nearby there is a shed with a corrugated roof on the left hand side of the road. Walk up the small road on the right hand side just before where you parked. There are some thatched cottages visible on the right. Walk into the grassy clearing on the left hand side of the road and continue over to the low-lying graves on your right in the field.*

MACDARA'S ANCIENT CELL CHURCH

In the far corner of this old graveyard lies the ivy-clad ruins of a very early Christian church that was named after the Aran saint Macdara. There is a beautiful oratory on a small island of Macdara off the Connemara coast where he lived too. The cell church once spawned a carving of a serpent which sadly has long disappeared. Adjacent to the church ruin is a a graveyard earmarked for children under the age of seven. They may not have received Communion rites, nor even have been baptized, and so were not considered fit for Christian burials. Such was the harsh thinking of the times. These oft forgotten, unmarked graveyards are scattered in isolated places throughout Ireland, and are known in Irish as "cillins". I witnessed a moving ceremony one cold winter's morn when the local priest lay prostrate on the ground, poignantly begging forgiveness for the cruel practice and ignorance of his antecedents. The woman who had asked him to create such a ceremony had placed white angels and pots of white chrysanthemums on each grave. The parishioners gathered round in respectful silence. One by one they called aloud the names of their own children who had died.

RESUME WHEN READY

Return uphill to the end of the road and turn right at the junction to return to where the staggered junction by the castle gates lies. This time carry on for Lisdoonvarna, and as you approach the town you will pass the award-winning Wild Honey Inn on your right. Turn right in the square and pass by the Hydro Hotel on your right. Stop and explore the town and visit the quaint architecture and landscape of the old spa – this is hidden in the landscaped hollow on the left hand side before the junction for Ennistymon and Corofin.

POINT L: LISDOONVARNA 53.030478, -9.289826   5.7 km

This tiny town becomes the world's centre for matchmaking in September! There is also in recent times a festival for gays, lesbians and transexuals at another time of year. This is a far cry from the genteel taking of the waters in Victorian times. The minerals were inferior in quality to spa towns elsewhere in Europe but they were ingeniously promoted in Victorian times, establishing it as a thriving Irish spa town! It really comes alive these years each September for matchmaking, thanks to further Irish ingenuity. Ireland's iconic folk singer Christy Moore has immortalized the town in his song Lisdoonvarna, where he frequently mentions the Craic, meaning the fine mixture of wit and chat and slight madness. This you find in abundance during the Match-making festival, not to be missed.

RESUME WHEN READY

Head for Ennistymon by turning right at the top of the street. As you leave the town you meet the R478 junction where you turn left onto the N67 going toward Ennistymon. You'll pass through Kilshanny where you can enjoy a warm welcome at the local pub, Kilshanny House on the left. A little further on the left you will see a signpost for a priory which belonged to the Augustinian monks who founded their only monastery in the Burren here. *After a sharp bend to the right, at the first crossroads, having crossed a small river, take the small road L5178 to the right. Almost immediately there is a farm track up to the right, belonging to Mr O'Dwyer. Park opposite his drive, pulling in off the road.*

POINT M: CEREMONIAL CAIRN 52.973351, -9.298924   8.3 km

CAIRN NEAR KILSHANNY *Photo by Kevin Lynch*

Walk to the bungalow and ask the owner for permission to enter his farm, for between the house and the river lies a giant cairn, as if standing guard over the land. It is long associated with battle and legends. This is Cairn Connaugtagh, a legendary burial mound in the townland of Ballydeely, named after one of Ireland's bravest warriors Daelach, son of the Fir Bolg chief Umor. Downstream the river bears this warrior's name. Here it is called the Dereen river. In another myth the Clare men defeated the Connaught men and buried the chiefs under the big cairn, although variations on the tale mention only one chieftain buried there. Then there is another story of three men from Loop Head on the coast south of here, successfully battling against the northern raiders at this spot.

In the early medieval period the ruling O'Connor clan of Corcamodruad inaugurated their chiefs here. It's really ancient name is 'Carn Mhic Tail'. None of this information prepared me for the overwhelming feeling the first sight of this massive cairn engendered in me. I would agree with the eminent archaeologist Carleton Jones that this was more than likely a prehistoric burial mound which was appropriated for inaugurating their chiefs upon, for assembling their tribes, for pronouncing the native Brehon laws, and for assembling before battle. It was used for instance in 1573 to assemble troops for a battle in which the O'Connors and O'Briens were on opposing sides!

A local romance written in 1750 by Comyn was roughly based on existing folklore. It mentions a formidable flesh-eating local sow that spawned four dragons who were reared by the red demon of Doo Lough past Milltown Malbay. In the O'Brien's ruling times their army is said to have chased a dragon up a valley in the Corcomroe district of the Burren and stoned it. The cairn here consists of those very stones, and this would mean it is likely the dragon lies buried beneath the cairn!

RESUME WHEN READY

Return to the N67 and turn right onto the main road toward Ennistymon.

POINT N: ENNISTYMON 52.943052, -9.292771   4.6 km

Pause in Ennistymon and explore this market town. Set besides the rapids of the Inagh River, it has a unique charm. At the top of the main street just beyond Supervalu, on the left hand side is an old Protestant church, outside of which stands a statue to Brian Merriman, a self-educated native poet and writer. He is looking down the main street of this old town. Merriman was an Irish poet and writer who lived from 1749-1780. He was a studious farmer who came from near Ennistymon and ended up leading a school in Limerick. His epic poem the Midnight Feast is comical and yet carries a serious message about the natural powers of women. It has been translated many times. The great poet of recent decades Seamus Heaney paid tribute to this man's work. Merriman's work has spawned regular winter schools and summer festivals and even websites.

ENNISTYMON FALLS

The Inagh rapids are best viewed from the Falls Hotel that is reached by walking through the lower end of the square and taking a lane past the library and small Steiner school. There are some beautiful old trees that line the approach to the spa hotel, an extended Georgian house where Dylan Thomas briefly lived. There was a castle owned by the O'Briens here in former times. Stand on the hotel steps and gaze out over the river to the hilltop graveyard. Perhaps that hill was an ancient ceremonial spot once. The path behind the hotel heads up to an enchanting ravine carved by a small tributary running through mature beeches. Known as the Glen, it is well worth a ramble.

RESUME WHEN READY

The final part of the return journey is made by turning right onto the main street and then taking the first right that crosses an old narrow bridge over the Falls on your right. Head back along the Inagh valley to Lahinch.

Lahinch   3.3 km

End of Lahinch Trail 2

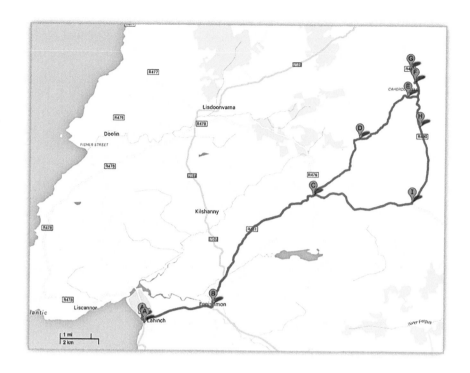

LAHINCH TRAIL 3

TOTAL DISTANCE ☞ 48.1 km

AUDIO FILE:

http://www.earthwise.me/product/burren-trails-audio/

POINT A: LAHINCH 52.934802, -9.344523

From Lahinch Promenade Car Park turn left and carefully join the N67 by continuing straight on passing the top of the main street. Follow this road inland a couple of miles. To your left winds the lovely Inagh river, apparently named after the ivy plant which is ubiquitous here. Some attribute the name to a local female saint. Since the Irish language is not used so widely nowadays, interpretation of places and rivers are open to various theories.

POINT B: ENNISTYMON 52.940828, -9.293711   4 km

The market town of Ennistymon has a wide square more typical of English settlements, but the small shops surrounding it were originally nearly all pubs, which was a very Irish thing indeed. In my teens I used to love going into this town from my grandparents' farm. I could chat with the colourful townspeople who often bid me sit down with them and listen to a tale or two. If it was a sunny afternoon they would pull out their 'sugauns' (hand made wicker chairs), puffing on their pipes or clicking on their crochet needles. I still love at times to sit and parly and watch the world go by. Horses and donkeys pulled open carts... such things are rare nowadays though only a few months ago I met a local farmer in one of the pubs who still rides a cart into town! The Falls Hotel offers a splendid view across the river and I was fortunate enough to attend a poignant funeral of the last of the local farmers to work the land solely with horses. This was Gus Queally from Aughtychristorie–his farm was truly magical with brass shining in the tackle shed, a pale blue half-door and deep window sills sparkling with fresh paint. I caught the tail end of this way of life. We may or may not have to wait a long time until such quality of life returns– when people will all look out for one another and will not judge you by your worldly possessions. Even the travellers who parked outside the cemetery on the hill were treated with respect to the best of my knowledge. By 'the travellers' I mean the culture formerly called 'the tinkers'. They used to call on my grandmother to get boiling water for their tea from her range, and ended up sharing tales. My own father was always on good terms with these people. Sadly their way of life has changed beyond recognition.

To visit the Falls Hotel on foot or driving, take the small road that leads from the square, past the library and the Rudolf Steiner School, both on your left. Go through the gates of the hotel and follow the driveway up. The river is on your left and there are several donkeys on the strip of land between the river and the wall. The entire walk is .6km.

RESUME WHEN READY

As you leave the town going uphill notice the Protestant church on your left with the statue outside of the late eighteenth century playwright and poet Brian Merriman. *A few miles on, the main road forks with a road going uphill to the right. Take this fork that leads to Kilfenora where you will be stopping in the square.*

POINT C: KILFENORA 52.99074, -9.215691   8.4 km

Kilfenora is famed for its ceilidh band that plays at country dances and festivals. Their lively tunes accompany "set dancers" who dance in quadrilles of four couples. There are a number of dances within a set that was traditionally danced in the open at crossroads following the harvest. It still occurs occasionally in rural parts of Ireland. The dancers move in quick steps to the music following a series of often complicated geometric patterns on the dance floor. It has been proved medically that such dancing helps reduce brain deterioration such as occurs in Alzheimers Disease, and a wider medical community in Europe is studying its benefits!

A thousand years ago Kilfenora was a strong centre of Celtic Christianity, within a wider context of rural democracy. Although St Fachtna had his monastery here in the sixth century, its true golden age was around 1050. The chief of the reigning 'Corcu Madruad' tribe in the Burren lived in the Kilfenora district where many magnificent ring forts graced the landscape. The high density of these cashels or forts is still visible on rises in the land round Kilfenora. Following the reform of the indigenous Irish Church in the twelfth century, which had become wealthy and intertwined with local ruling families, the Roman Catholic Church ensured that all religious establishments paid their dues directly to dioceses led by archbishops, based in five newly created regional centres. Sounds familiar? The dioceses demanded ten percent of all local produce, a proportion of which was then forwarded to Rome. Inevitably the chief's land became a substantial part of the Diocese of Kilfenora in the twelfth century.

The land was further subdivided into east and west, where the O'Loughlins gained the barony of the Burren in the east, while the O'Connors gained the barony of Corcomroe in the west. (Ironically the Burren as we know it nowadays is more associated with the Corcomroe barony than the old Burren barony, which is nevertheless still geologically part of the Burren.) Baronies were subdivided into bailes, parishes, and townlands. The latter were the tiniest divisions, often occupied by single family names.

Perhaps to commemorate this reform of power distribution, a cluster of seven very distinct twelfth century high crosses were placed in the vicinity of the cathedral. The present church was built between 1189 and 1200. The carvings on the crosses show appointed bishops, sometimes with the older style bishop alongside or below the new style of bishop. Only six crosses remain and only one is in its original position, 200 yards west of the cathedral. The other five have been brought into the north wing of the cathedral for protection from the elements. The most interesting feature

DOORTY CROSS
SHOWING BISHOP
WITH TAU STAFF

is on the Doorty Cross, which seems to mark the divisions between the Celtic and tribal-led diocese and the new centralized Roman model that began in 1152. This cross depicts a bishop clutching a Tau cross, or T-shaped cross, as his staff. Such a symbol stems from the eastern Orthodox tradition, linking into a pre-Roman theology which I believe was prevalent here and in the Aran Islands. Later we shall see a most interesting example of the Tau cross on the Ennis tour.

There was another church with a hospital on private land in the vicinity. Kilfenora Cathedral had an oak ceiling that was painted with small stars on a blue background, still visible until the end of the nineteenth century. In the first half of the thirteenth century the cathedral became the centre for a school of masons known as "School of the West".

To view the old cathedral with its collection of early decorative crosses, face away from the Burren Centre in the square and walk left down a side road alongside the walled enclosure. Enter through a low doorway in the wall of the graveyard and walk right round the cathedral to view the crosses in the new extension. One monument remains free-standing in its original position in a field 200 yards to the west—to reach it go through the graveyard and out the medieval gateway. Walk down the lane and climb over the stile to enter the field where the high cross stands ahead of you, on a natural elevation formed by some low-lying cliffs.

If you continue past the doorway in the wall by which you originally entered the cathedral you can walk to the end of the short lane. It passes the site of a well that has disappeared (Tobar Dein), and ends at a well dedicated to St Fachtna. The enclosure was built in 1687 and has been lovingly restored for local benefit. Thankfully there has been a revival of interest in holy wells in Ireland, and this area is no exception. Wells are seen as sanctuaries within our busy world. Interestingly when I moved over to Ireland in late 2008 I found myself visiting many of the earliest ecclesiastical sites, still complete with wells, although many other wells in open countryside have long disappeared.

RESUME WHEN READY

Returning to the square take the road to the left signposted to Lisdoonvarna, just past Linnanes, a small pub that was opened when its owner won the lottery and decided to open a traditional pub for a novelty! *Once on this road almost immediately take a road to the right which leads towards Noughaval. The turning is just past a housing estate on the right, and has a cycling trail sign at the junction.* On the farms along this road substantial old cashels or forts remain visible, all in various states of decay. Overall in the Burren there are over 450 ring forts and some here are most impressive in scale. They capture a time of posterity that imparts its own atmosphere on the landscape. These ring forts remained under Gaelic control until the 1750s. The high walls of Ballykinvarga and its surrounding cashels reflect a longer period of habitation than elsewhere, and they also reflect the significant wealth of the chief who lived there. If you wish to walk across the fields to visit one do ask locally to gain permission for access, and make sure you close all gates behind you. *Shortly before your next official stop there is a road to your left signposted to Ballyvaughan. Do not take this but continue straight on. Park on front of the present day church on the right in Noughaval.* Then walk on until you reach the gate into the old graveyard beyond. Notice the base of the old market cross outside the gate.

This site was an important place of pilgrimage in the land-scape. It once had a round tower on it (others are at Kil-naboy and old Raha Church locally). The pilgrims would have journeyed from Kilfenora via Noughaval to the coast at Newquay. There was a well beyond the old church, close to the road. It is dedicated to the founder of Noughaval, St Mo-gua, whose feast day is one week after St Colman's in Feb-ruary. This means that if the pilgrims set off from here on St Mogua's feast day on 3ʳᵈ February they would have reached St Colman's dedicatory area by the end of a week. Probably they stopped off at St Colman's Well above Oughtmama as featured in the Kinvara trail. Noughaval's ecclesiastical site may be the earliest Christian site in the Burren. We can tell that by the large stones seen in the south wall of the old church. Like many churches that have been rebuilt in later centuries in the Burren, there was an earlier church on the site, and the simplest evidence for this lies in the large Cy-clopean masonry in the south wall, where the original door would have led into a small, rectangular cell church built in the Golden Ratio proportions of 13 feet by 21 feet. This pro-portion was known to facilitate deep meditation and elevate thoughts. The absence of windows also would have led the thoughts inward.

A simple stone mound to the south of the church is known as a "leacht" in Irish. The antecedent's bones may well have been buried here when the early Christians came from an-other site. I have seen similar mounds in the far north of Scotland. Archaeologists assume they are either open air al-tars or burial mounds. It may have been both! It is again an indicator of the site's early associations with pilgrimages. I am inclined to think they primarily served as preaching bases, much in the way that sacred trees and standing stones used to act as bases for gathering for prayer in the early Christian times in Celtic countries. Perhaps the earliest monks came here and preached before there was a proper church built on the site. A Celtic cross can be seen on top of the mound.

OLD CROSS AT NOUGHAVAL

There was a circular wall round the whole site which you can still see in the southwest. Carlton Jones is an Irish archaeologist whom I much admire. He feels that the circular wall may have been demarcating an old monastic boundary. It is hard to tell as many churches in the Burren and elsewhere in Ireland were built on top of prehistoric, circular enclosures (raths). The chapel you see inside the graveyard is a mortuary chapel for the O'Davorens who ran an important law school at Cahermacnaughten nearby. We see the remains of their law school on the Ballyvaughan trail that follows this. Before leaving, pause to view the multitude of small upright stones that strew the graveyard. These markers were often placed where victims of the potato blight famine had been buried, according to one local O'Loughlin.

Noughaval was once an important medieval settlement though the original market cross has disappeared, leaving only a stump behind.

RESUME WHEN READY

Continue on the road you are on, and after a couple of kilometres you get a fine view of a large cairn inland on the right hand side. Whilst there was a public path into the cairn in recent times it has been removed by the landowner, so if you want to view it you **must** make local enquiries. There is a magical cairn you can visit on the Lahinch Trail 2. *Just before reaching the end of the road, there is a lay-by on the right. You know if you have gone too far as after the lay-by the road swings sharply to the right, before descending to join a junction with a minor road you can see below you on the left. Pull over into the lay-by to hear about Poulawack.*

POINT E: POULAWACK CAIRN 53.039355, 9.152008　　　　2.8 km

Poulawack Cairn was of great significance in the prehistoric landscape. It began as a cist burial on a small natural rise around 3350 BC, thus dating it to Neolithic times. Many people, animals and artefacts were placed inside two compartments, including a large boar's tusk, an infant and a middle-aged couple. The second phase began around 2000BC when three more burial cists were built inside the same cairn, containing human bones of several individuals. Then around 1500 BC, the cairn was heightened by one metre and more unburnt human bones were placed in yet more cists, some of which contained burnt or cremated bones. A crouched inhumation in a rough grave was added too. Like the famous dolmen at Poulnabrone nearby, this cairn was in use throughout the early Neolithic, late Neolithic period and early Bronze Age.

There is not much else to see at Poulawack other than a massive pile of stones, but it is interesting to know that the place was so significant in ancient times.

RESUME WHEN READY

Continue down the road as far as the bottom of the hill. Turn right onto the minor road the L5904. Almost immediately turn left onto the main road the R480 signposted for Ballyvaughan, and head for the famous Poulnabrone dolmen, a major tourist icon for Ireland. This is an intriguing landscape with collapsed caves and river systems, wedge tombs and wells that are hard to find at times. En route you can pay a visit to the Caherconnell ring fort for light refreshments and an archaeological tour of their fort.

POINT F: CAHER CONNEL FORT 53.046167, -9.137589   2.4 km

You will notice this visitor centre easily due to its array of national flags on high flagpoles. Pull into its car park on the left. It is a well-preserved fort conveniently spotted from the road.

Other forts take longer to reach, and as usual there would be the problem of accessing private land, as footpaths are very few in Ireland compared to their neighbouring countries.

RESUME WHEN READY

Continue for 800 metres and park at the car park on your right to visit the famous dolmen of Poulnabrone.

POINT G: POULNABRONE DOLMEN   53.050662, -9.145989   800 m

POULNABRONE TOMB

The interesting fact about dolmen sitings is that archaeologists have more or less agreed that rather than mere burial places these dolmens acted as focal gathering points in the landscape. This site means 'Hole of the Sorrows'. An excavation before a repair to this monument revealed that 21 corpses had been transferred to the tomb after their flesh had decayed. In very early times bodies were left out for birds of prey to devour. I wonder if this is what happened here. The burials took place around 3200BC, which was about 600 years after farming began in the Burren. The actual tomb may be older. The exact reasons for burying people here are left to the imagination, but it followed about 600 years of farming in the Burren. In the early Bronze Age the remains of a newborn baby was placed in a small cist just in front of the main chamber. The practice of inserting new burials became fairly common between 1750 and 1420 BC. The site is indisputably a significant place in the landscape as is evidenced by a network of localized leys, and a larger ley system, traversing it. When I dowse these leys, or energy lines, even from a distance I can detect them as they are powerful.

RESUME WHEN READY

Turn left out the car park, returning the way you came . Pass the crossroads where you joined this road when you drove down from Noughaval. The road you are on now leads you past Carron Church on the left hand side. Park outside the hedge and wall of a grey bungalow opposite. Cross the road and climb the stile into a field that the church is situated in. There is a small decorated gate further back.

OLD WARRIOR FACE, CARRON

Look for the warrior's face set into the low section of the external wall of this nave. There used to be a carving of a king and queen's face carved here also. Carron means "cairn" or "heap of stones". It was probably named after a small cairn here in the graveyard, around which the bearers would parade coffins before burial. This tradition hints again at a link to a pre-Christian rite.

RESUME WHEN READY

Continue straight on. After passing a turning for Carran village on the right, drive on until the road meets a T junction. Leamaneh Castle looms large on the right. Turn right and park on front of the castle if you can. You are facing in the right direction to continue your journey then.

POINT I: LEAMANEH CASTLE 52.990817, -9.1379   4 km

LEAMANEH CASTLE

This is a fifteenth century tower house to which a seventeenth century manor house was added. There was once a formal walled garden, a fish pond, a summer house and even a turret walk along the wall to enjoy views of the garden from. A sturdy high wall in the distance kept deer in, and Leamaneh/ or Leamenagh, actually means " deer's leap" in Irish! Beyond all this lies a cashel 'Caherscebeen'. Leamaneh survives because its owner 'Maire Rua', or red Mary, married a Cromwellian in order to retain the estate within the O'Brien family she had married into. The O'Briens had built this castle at the confluence of three major territories-those of the O'Loughlins, whose main castle was at Cregans we pass on the Ballyvaughan trail; the O'Deas of Inchiquin on the Ennis trail; and the O'Connors of Corcomroe in the west, on the Kinvara trail. The ancient main roads in the cardinal directions intersect here, so it was strategically placed indeed.

RESUME WHEN READY

Follow the road back to Kilfenora and then carry on for Ennisty-mon. Turn right over the low old bridge to Lahinch and your destination.

Lahinch Promenade   18.2 km

End of Lahinch Trail 3

BALLYVAUGHAN TRAIL 1

TOTAL DISTANCE ☞ 38.4 km

AUDIO FILE:

http://www.earthwise.me/product/burren-trails-audio/

Introduction

POINT A: BALLYVAUGHAN 53.11546, -9.149262

Despite the distracting plethora of signage on the approaches to Ballyvaughan, there is a definite air of tranquillity and even other-worldliness to this pocket of the world. I think this is partly due to a major pattern of strong, spiritual ley lines culminating here. Ballyvaughan is the nearest town to the central core ley line of an 'earth grid' I write about in my books Spirit of the Burren and Essence of the Burren, which incidentally are for sale in the tourist information centre in Ballyvaughan. Speaking of spirit, there is a genuine old pub that specializes in whiskey varieties near the quayside in Ballvaughan. O'Loughlin's displays its opening hours by personal note on the door. With its small rooms, dark panelling and convivial ambience, even a teatotaller might find it relaxing.

WHISKEY SHOP IN BALLYVAUGHAN

Walk out along the row of cottages facing the waterfront until you reach the last building, which was built in 1790 to accommodate coastal security officers. This was just in time for guarding against a possible invasion from France during the Wars of Coalition that lasted until 1815. Now called The Tea and Garden Rooms, its centre piece is a very large table sagging with their display of scrumptious homemade cakes.

You can sit out in the perfumed conservatory or on one of the patios in the walled gardens. About a kilometre further out on the coast road is 'An Fulacht Fia', a restaurant that is reasonably priced and has a good reputation. Fulacht fia means a 'burnt mound', an archaeological term for crescent-shaped mounds of spent hot stones, formed presumably when the heated stones were extracted and piled up, after having effectively boiled the water placed in cooking pits. Opinion is divided as to the exact purpose of these pits. They range from cooking pits to foot saunas! There are many scattered throughout the Burren and in particular along its coastal stretches. Another restaurant I know and like in Ballyvaughan is l'Arco. It is accessed through a main archway in the main street beside a large gift shop. This restaurant offers genuine Italian cooking.

RESUME WHEN READY

Before we over-indulge *let's drive on by taking the road signposted for Lisdoonvarna at the main junction in the village.* Lisdoonvarna itself is covered in the Lahinch Section Trail 2. *Only a few kilometres out of Ballyvaughan there is a fork in the road. Take the left fork where Ailwee Cave and Caherconnel Fort are clearly signposted on a brown tourist sign. This is the R480 to Kilfenora and Ennis. Soon, on the left hand side of the road you will find a large entrance road to Ailwee Cave.* A hidden treasure lies half way up the slopes. The impressive Birds of Prey centre situated in the first car park to your left is well worth a visit.

STOP B: BIRDS OF PREY CENTRE 53.090571, -9.146039   3.8 km

RESUME WHEN READY

Across the road and beside the farm shop there is a footpath leading up through the woods to the main visitor centre for the cave. The sign is well visible and says it will take 5 minutes. There are some very interesting woodcraft demonstrations in the woodland too. Alternatively you can drive up to the top car park in order to visit Ailwee Cave.

STOP C: AILWEE CAVE 53.090313, -9.143128   450 m

The cave is relatively short by world standards but is nevertheless Ireland's largest publicly accessible cave, and is well presented. It offers you an excellent overview on how these caves were formed in the Burren. Ailwee Cave is set within Ailwee Mountain, which, with Slieve Elva to the west, constitutes the main mountains in the Burren. Slieve Elva is best approached in the second section of the Ballvaughan tour.

RESUME WHEN READY

Drive down the hillside. Turn left out the exit toward Ennis on the R480. Drive slowly because after only a few metres there is a set of gates on the left. Park in the lay-by well away from the gates to this private home. Just across the road on the right hand side, beside the road signs, is a wooden stile leading into a massive earthen works.

VIEW OF BALLYALBAN

This earthen fort is most impressive. There are only a few such works in the Burren and these are mainly in lowland areas. This was a fort which used to protect cattle against wild animals such as wolves, and possibly against marauding invaders too. Tree roots intricately lace the large circular ridge.

RESUME WHEN READY

Continue carefully on the road until you come to the first steep bend to the left. Nearly opposite on the right is a farm gate, and just beyond this is a lay-by where you must pull in and park.

Walk over the stile in the wall and follow the path up through a pleasant hazel thicket.

POINT E: CAHERMOR FORT 53.085918, -9.163846   650 m

CAHERMOR

MEDIEVAL GATEWAY TO CAHERMOR

Two sentry areas either side of the entrance create a unique identity for this well-preserved stone fort. You can see the stone outlines of many smaller homes within the fort, and in places the protective wall is still quite high. The place appropriately means Big Fort in Irish. There more than likely was a relatively large population living here, living off domestic and wild animals, hazelnuts and even shellfish from the nearby coast.

RESUME WHEN READY

Continue on the road, passing a large lay-by at Ballyalban viewpoint. Three km from the last stop, you come to a small lay-by on the left where you can park. There is a gated track leading up the slopes at an acute angle to the road, which it is not visible until you park. Walk to the next gate just beyond the lay-by on the same side.

POINT F: GLENINSHEEN GORGET 53.067523, -9.150166   2.9 km

To the right of the path beyond this gate lies a large stone engraved with a plaque depicting the gold torc, or gorget, that was found in the vicinity by a dog who was walking with Paddy Nolan, a local shepherd, in 1939. This fine gold object is more commonly associated with the high quality gold and bronze finds of that period around the Shannon estuary. It remains a bit of a mystery as to why it was left here in a crevice in the rocks. It appears to have been deposited for safe-keeping! This brilliant ceremonial object from the late Bronze Age is now on display in the Museum of Irish Antiquities.

RESUME WHEN READY

*Drive on slowly and as you draw level with the first dia-
mond-shaped road sign on the right, look over the wall to the
left of you* and you will see a marvellous specimen of a
cist grave. These are the most common type of prehistoric
graves in the region, but there are quite a few dolmens, or
portal tombs too. *As you drive on through quite dramatic topography you will soon reach the main car park on the left for
Poulnabrone, an iconic dolmen you pass on the same side.* This
is a portal tomb. Other types of tomb found in Ireland are
known as court tombs, passage tombs and wedge tombs (cist
graves), the latter being numerous in the Burren.

POINT G: POULNABRONE DOLMEN   2.4 km

POULNABRONE AT DAWN

Poulnaborne means "Hole of Sorrows", and was constructed around 3200 BC. An excavation undertaken prior to repairing Poulnabrone revealed that after about 600 years of
farming activity in the area, 21 corpses were transferred to
the tomb, once their flesh had decayed. The tomb itself may
be older than these finds. The exact reason for this Neolithic ritual burial is unknown. Then in the early Bronze Age

the remains of a newborn baby was placed in a small cist just in front of the main chamber. The practice of inserting new burials became fairly commonplace between 1750 and 1420 BC. The site is indisputably a significant place in the landscape as is evidenced by a network of localized leys set within a larger ley system.

RESUME WHEN READY

Turn left out of the car park and continue for about .4 km. On the road on the right hand side is a visitor centre distinguished by a series of raised flags on poles..

POINT H: CAHERCONNELL FORT 53.043587,-9.138249   800 m

Here you can visit the ancestral cashel, or fort, of the Connells. Archaeological finds on site make for an interesting tour. You can also have a light lunch and browse their book and gift shop. Return to your vehicle.

RESUME WHEN READY

About 1.5 km further up the road take the first turn to the right, signposted to Poulawack Cairn. Your route continues by forking off shortly to the right. However, if you took the left fork uphill towards Noughaval and look right across the landscape, you may sight the ancient cairn of Poulawack as it stands on an elevated site. Pause somewhere convenient to listen.

POULAWACK CAIRN.

In recent times this cairn on private land has become quite inaccessible. Even if you reached it, there is not much to see apart from a massive pile of stones. However, it is worth knowing that this cairn was highly significant in ancient times. It began as a cist burial on a small natural rise around 3350 BC dating it to a similar Neolithic period as Poulnabrone. Many people, animals and other artefacts were placed inside two compartments, intriguingly including a large boar's tusk, an infant and a middle-aged couple. The second phase began around 2000BC when three more burial cists were built inside the same cairn, containing both burnt and unburnt human bones of several individuals. Then in around 1500 BC the cairn was heightened by one metre and more unburnt human bones were placed in yet more cists, and a crouched inhumation in a rough grave was added as well. This time some of the cists contained burnt or cremated bones too. Like the famous dolmen at Poulnabrone, this cairn was in use over the early Neolithic, late Neolithic period and early Bronze Age.

POULAWACK CAIRN IN DISTANCE

RESUME WHEN READY

Assuming you don't take the high road toward Noughaval, you are now one the small road that goes downhill at the first fork to the right, fairly near the junction with the main R480. This leads you through an atmospheric green valley, where a hidden cave in the limestone cliffs to the right carries the legendary title "Cave of the Wild Horses". It is not a very exciting cave to enter but its haunting name suggests the quiet valley has some subtle energies. *At the end of the road through this small valley turn right toward Kilfenora and Lis-doonvarna and head northwards. After just over a kilometre you may spot another ruined fort or cashel on the left, close to a farmhouse in open farmland. You are allowed to visit this fort but parking facilities are nil. Park beyond the farm drive beside the fort – but be careful not to block any gates.*

POINT I: CAHERMACNAGHTON STONE FORT AND EARLY LAW
SCHOOL 53.049469, -9.195954   9.4 km

Compared to Caherconnell Fort, this homestead or fort lies in a far more dilapidated state. However, like Poulawack, this was once a significant social hub. It may have been occupied as early as 500 AD, and has continued in use for over 1000 years. Note the medieval gateway. The ancient Davoren Law School was in operation here until around 1500, teaching their students the old ways inherent in the Brehon Laws, which reinforced fairness. Rather than punishing the offenders, the law school trained people to oversee that offenders awarded damages to their victims. The law-making clan of Davorens helped prolong a sense of ethics and justice in the local pop-ulation too, and this, in my mind, more than justifies them having a special mortuary chapel at Noughaval, seen on La-hinch Trail 2. (It can be reached if you continued on the high road past Poulawack mentioned earlier.) The early–late Medieval laws were very detailed and enlightened and even now they have attracted an annual summer school in the locality to discuss their ethics! I am reminded of Adamnan's laws in Scotland. He was the successor to the Irish born prince Columba who ruled Iona Abbey. Adamnan died at Dull, their sister monastery, in mainland Perthshire. His laws were fair to women and sowed the seeds of liberty, freedom and equality that later became the main tenets of Scottish law. Sadly, Ireland did not follow in Scotland's wake and instead became more divorced from its old wise ways as centuries of English occupation wore on. In 1675 the O'Davorens were still living within the fort. A part of the Book of the Genealogies of Ireland written from 1585 onwards was recorded here.

RESUME WHEN READY

Continue on the road north and after 2 km you reach the main Lisdoonvarna-Ballyvaughan road where you will turn right down Corkscrew Hill. Pause at this junction by parking in the lay-by on the left.

Across the road from this junction in the wilderness of this mountainside remains a blessed tree of Brigid, accompanied by her knee indentations on the rocky ground. This is where the saint is said to have walked all the way from Galway. There is an old medieval road still visible leading to it. You can discover the actual whereabouts if you use Tim Robinson's maps. There is a scattering of blessed trees between here and the coast heading back to Galway, and in this case the tree has been ascribed to Brigid. This pinnacle saint is said to have walked here from Galway on a pilgrimage. She is much revered by a wide cross-section of society to this day.

ST BRGID'S KNEES BELOW HOLY BUSH

RESUME WHEN READY

Turn back towards Ballyvaughan which is down the hill toward the sea. As you descend the hill with some breathtaking views, be prepared for some real hairpin bends as this is Corkscrew Hill after all! Do drive with care! After the hairpin bends, on the lower slopes, Gregan's hotel on the right offers one of the most refined pit stops in County Clare, let alone the Burren! Enter the gates of the hotel marked with the hotel's name and journey up the driveway to the parking area.

ROSE GARDEN IN GREGAN'S HOTEL

Its lovely gardens complete with wilderness areas, a stream and pool peak in a rose garden set in the shape of a Celtic cross. The rose garden is on front of the hotel and centres round a gyroscope set on a plinth. It is dedicated to the owner's youngest son who died tragically. Its multi lingual message is very poignant. Lunch is an option here for those who like to travel in style!

RESUME WHEN READY

Leave the hotel, turning right out of the exit. Almost opposite the exit to the hotel on the left hand side, lies Gregan's Castle. The privately owned L-shaped castle and grounds once belonged to the powerful O'Loughlin clan, while later owners, the Martyns, lived in another castle which lies in ruins in the woods.

Continue a few more km on the Ballyvaughan road, and at the first junction turn sharp left onto the L10282. Now you are travelling close to the main east-west axis ley of the main pattern of ley lines in the Burren. The river Bourney rises to the surface here and creates a verdant green valley.

There are two churches on this road. *The first turning on the left leads to a large parish church built in 1795.* If the gate is closed do not enter—if the road is open the owner does not mind you visiting the old church and adjacent rath.

RESUME WHEN READY

STOP K: GLENARAHA PARISH CHURCH 53.089901,-9.17672   2.8 km

Since the church is large it can give you an idea of the pre-Famine and pre-Emmigration population density in the valley. Step into the trees to the left of the church and view the remains of a massive earthen fort, again hinting at higher historical populations in this valley.

RESUME WHEN READY

*Return to the byroad and turn left to continue. After 1.7km you come to another short avenue to the left–*this takes you Rathbourney Church, high above the river by that name.

POINT L: RATHBOURNEY CHURCH 53.093824, -9.200515   2 km

The site hints at an earlier religious function, for it abuts an unexcavated mound at its eastern end. Mysteriously there is no door into the mound from the church, although an earlier cell church might have been within it. Originally it might have been a rath. There is a baptismal font lying in the grass among gravestones to the southwest of the church. Some call this a bullaun stone or basin stone, allegedly used for pounding herbs and grains, though I have seen similar ones identified as very early baptismal and blessing fonts in highland Scotland.

BULLAUN STONE WITH MOUND AND CHURCH IN BACKGROUND

I love this valley with its air of timeless peace. There is a most interesting legend of a sacred cow, Glasha, I will relate on a Gort section tour. Her hoof marks are commemorated in the hills above this valley, some distance away from her usual haunt on Slieve na Glasha.

RESUME WHEN READY

Return the road you drove up and at the end take the L10283 road immediately to the left. After you see a small road to the left with a sign for The Waters, you are almost upon your next stop on the right, Newtown Castle, one of the few round towers in the Burren. Drive into the gateway and park on the left in the car park.

POINT M: NEWTOWN CASTLE / BURREN COLLEGE OF ART
    53.105465, -9.169148   3.7 km

The small castle might have been built with defence, rather than domestic comforts, in mind. Now it is part of an active arts foundation that has a small café on its premises too. You may visit the castle if open (entrance is free).

RESUME WHEN READY.

Continue on the L10282 and take the next small road on the right that runs parallel to the college driveway down to the main road to Ballyvaughan. Turn left at the end and head back to Ballyvaughan.

Ballyvaughan 53.118345,-9.150635 2.9 km

End of Ballyvaughan Trail 1

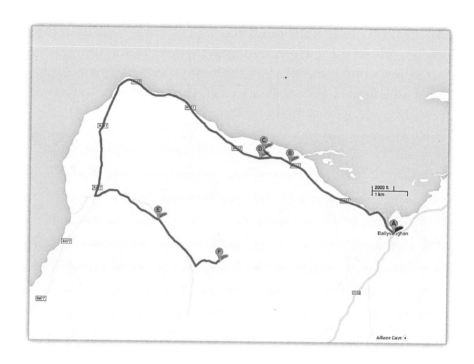

BALLYVAUGHAN TRAIL 2

TOTAL DISTANCE ☞ 35.7 km

AUDIO FILE:

http://www.earthwise.me/product/burren-trails-audio/

POINT A: BALLYVAUGHAN 53.11546, -9.149262

Despite the distracting plethora of signage on the approaches to Ballyvaughan, there is a definite air of tranquillity and even other-worldliness to this pocket of the world. I think this is partly due to a major pattern of strong, spiritual ley lines culminating here. Ballyvaughan is the nearest town to the central core ley line of an 'earth grid' I write about in my book Spirit of the Burren which is for sale in the tourist information centre in Ballyvaughan. Speaking of spirit, there is a genuine old pub that specializes in whiskey varieties near the quayside in Ballvaughan.

INTERIOR OF O'LOUGHLIN'S PUB

O'Loughlins displays its opening hours by personal note on the door. With its small rooms, dark panelling and convivial ambience even a teatotaller would find it relaxing. Walk out along the row of cottages facing the waterfront until you reach the last building which was built in 1790 to accommodate coastal security officers. This was just in time for guarding against a possible invasion from France during the Wars of Coalition that lasted until 1815. Now called The Tea and

Garden Rooms its centre piece is a very large table sagging with their display of scrumptious homemade cakes. You can sit out in the conservatory or better still on one of the patios in the walled gardens. About a kilometre further out on the coast road is *An Fulacht Fia*, a restaurant that is reasonably priced and has a good reputation. Fulacht fia means a 'burnt mound', an archaeological term for crescent-shaped mounds of spent hot stones, formed presumably when the heated stones were extracted and piled up, after having effectively boiled the water placed in cooking pits. Opinion is divided as to the exact purpose of these pits. They range from cooking pits to foot saunas! There are many scattered throughout the Burren and in particular along its coastal stretches. Another restaurant I know and love is l'Arco in Ballyvaughan, that is accessed through a main archway in the main street beside a large gift shop. This restaurant offers genuine Italian cooking.

RESUME WHEN READY

STARTING POINT Start out from the tourist information /gift shop in the main street at the back of the supermarket car park in Ballyvaughan 53.118345,-9.146145. Turn right and then right again so you are on the coast road heading towards Black Head to the west. After about four km on the left hand side you cannot miss a large artefact with pinnacles. This is the Pinnacle Well, much admired for its decorative stone covering. Stop here and listen.

PINNACLE WELL

The well was built in 1860 in the Gothic style to cover the spring, as it was the reserve water supply for Ballyvaughan in times of drought. Many ley lines are in close proximity to this well. One leyline runs directly behind the well. If you walk back a little and take the verdant boreen, or small road, down to the shoreline you can go foraging along the coast for seafood. Enjoy the marine environs of shore, shingle ridges and marshy land that lie in close proximity here. There are lobsters in the pools and small sea shrimps in the shallow waters, as well as the deliciously edible samphire and other sea vegetables. The Rine, the narrow spit of land projecting far into the bay, is a haven for migrating birds and seals.

RESUME WHEN READY

Continue west on the coast road and take the next public turning on the right. Drive on to the end of this small road, where there is a small area for parking. It is best to take the opportunity now to turn your car around to face your exiting direction if you have room to do so.

POINT C: GLENINAGH CASTLE AND HOLY CROSS WELL
53.136666, -9.205667   1 km

GLENINAGH WELL

Walk through the gate and head across the field seawards to view Gleninagh Castle that was once owned by the ruling O'Loughlins. Now managed by the Office of Public Works, the sixteenth century castle contains a finely preserved example of an L plan tower, a design shared by many Scottish castles. The O'Loughlins controlled much of north Clare until the nineteenth century. Although originally they lost it to British ownership, they eventually repossessed it in the mid 17th century after Cromwell had invaded Ireland. They remained there until at least 1840. Some interior alterations were made over the centuries. Nevertheless the exterior remains pretty intact and is interesting. There is an internal spiral stairway and an entrance contained within the projecting wing. Circular projections protect three corners, and even over the doorway there are defensive projections. On the seaward side are the garderobes that let out directly onto the wall. It has changed hands a few times, until the local owners the O'Donohues handed it over the Office of Public Works to maintain.

The fields surrounding this castle, so romantically positioned on the shoreline, are well worth exploring. Nearby there is a grass mound concealing a lime kiln complete with kiln door facing seaward, and a flue at the top. There are pits of blackened stones to be found that suggest there were fuluchta fia here too—these proliferate along the shore of the Burren and were either cooking pits using hot stones from the fires to boil fish and meat in, or they may even have been communal foot baths! You can take your pick of the current theories. The sea defence wall is marvellously constructed by hand. Close to the castle lies Gleninagh Well. Further on from the castle in a southerly direction lies a well-preserved medieval church ruins.

To reach it, drive back to the main road and turn right. Continue on a short distance and park on the left before an old building which lies past a bungalow. Across the road is a brown tourist sign for Gleninagh Church, almost hidden by foliage – a very pleasant short walk takes you to the church, which is most sensitively maintained.

POINT D: GLENINAGH CHURCH 53.134362, -9.207254   650 m

SIGN FOR GLENINAGH CHURCH

RESUME WHEN READY.

Now continue round the main headland at Black Head where inland waters from the Slieve Aughty Hills, east of the Burren, weave their way under the limestone and emerge here. Fish like to feed in areas where freshwater meets saltwater and there are plenty of mackerel to be caught here. Feel the full extent of the Atlantic breeze as you breathe in the fresh air, being mindful that there are mythical sites in the hills above you to explore if you wish. These hills carry legends of Diarmid and Grainne the famous lovers in romantic myth. They were chased by Seefin the favourite hound of Finn McCool, Grainne's jilted husband. The cairns above are named after princes of the more ancient "Fir Bolg", and even the mythical hound!

Take the first turning on the left after you reach Fanore and leave behind the bushes that line the road: look out for this turning that joins the road the other side of a small stone bridge over the river. Take this road past the old church of St Patricks on the right. You are now travelling up the so-called Kyber Pass! If you prefer, you can continue first a short distance on the main road to Fanore where you can avail yourself of lunch in upmarket Vasco's, or the local's O'Donohue's pub.

THE CAHER VALLEY

Like the Rathbourney river on the other Ballyvaughan trail, the Caher river is one of those rare rivers that surfaces in the Burren. In fact, this is the only Burren river that runs above ground from source to the sea. There are many underground rivers that carry away the rainfall almost as fast as it falls. Various topical historical remains lie up the tracks to your left off the road. In a remote spot further back into the lee of these hills there was a "still", where poteen or illegal liquor was made. One has to remember that there was a lot of unfair prohibition laid down by the ruling classes here then. There is no track to it but it can be spotted on Tim

Robinson's hand drawn map of the Burren, if you have one. His well-crafted map be purchased in Ballyvaughan Tourist Information centre and elsewhere.

Continue up the Caher Valley. "Caher" means fort, and there are many forts overlooking the appropriately named Caher river. It was in this valley that the writer John ODonohue returned to dwell – after he was born and raised here, John went on to become a priest. He then became a highly successful and eloquent writer on the spirituality of nature when he left the priesthood. His most famous book is Anam Cara, which means "Loved One". He constantly referenced his native Burren. He used to offer Easter Mass outdoors at sunrise at the ruined Cistercian abbey of Corcomroe, which is a little north of here on the Kinvara trail. He was astute in his criticisms of the Roman Catholic church and was a spiritual, rather than a religious, leader. At 52 years of age he passed into the other realm suddenly in his sleep. That was in 2008.

Just before a stone bridge lies a traditional cottage on the right, with adjoining gardens. They are open to the public by appointment only.

However, part of the award-winning garden can be enjoyed from the roadside looking from the small bridge that overlooks it.

GARDEN AT CAHER BRIDGE

RESUME WHEN READY

Drive on until you reach a road to the right. You will have passed an old penal chapel on the right hand side on the way (Catholics had to pray in secret during the fifteenth and sixteenth centuries when it was forbidden by the British to hold their services. Priests faced the death penalty when they gave Mass.). *Do not take the right hand turn but carry on and almost immediately there is a rough road to the left sign-posted The Burren Way. Turn left and park here at the side of the quiet track. Walk on.* There are marvellous views of the Atlantic afforded on the ascent to Caheranadurrish Fort. After about a kilometre of uphill walking, you will see the old fort on the right hand side, inside which the locals had concealed both a Mass house and a "shibeen", the latter an Irish word describing a secret drinking house, often used mainly for imbibing home-made illicit whiskey. The still in the hills nearby was no doubt in trade with this shibeen.

STOP F: CAHERANADURRISH FORT WITH MASS HOUSE AND SHIBEEN INSIDE 53.108221, -9.224249   2.5km

OLD SHIBEEN WITHIN FORT

So, here in this remote place, lay both the illegal church and illegal pub: the backbone of old Irish life. The shibeen was a low lying building with a double door entrance to accommodate the crowds that frequented this off-the-beaten track establishment! The harsh conditions of the times would have been softened with the 'water of life', as whiskey was called.

RESUME WHEN READY

Return to the junction and walk back a short distance. Turn up the first road on your left. This was the road you passed on the right coming up the road earlier. You can see an old chapel on the right hand side as you cross the bridge near the junction. Take the small track to the right after the bridge over the river Rathbouney, tucked in on the right hand side. There is an even smaller track just before this track and it leads to a holy well. Fermoyle Chapel contains a simple altar slab and bullaun stone. Bullaun stones are individually placed stones with single depressions in them. Some believe they were used for baptism or healing purposes, using the rainwater that gathered in them – others think they may have been used in grinding corn. Above the chapel lies the cillin for non-baptized children. I would imagine many of these children died young in the area due to malnutrition.

RESUME WHEN READY

Collect your car where you parked it and return to the main road at the bottom of the Caher Valley and. Turn right and head back down the coast road *where you can drop into Ballyvaughan and some legal whiskey perhaps!*

Ballyvaughan 53.118345, -9.150635 17.4 km

End of Ballyvaughan Trail 2

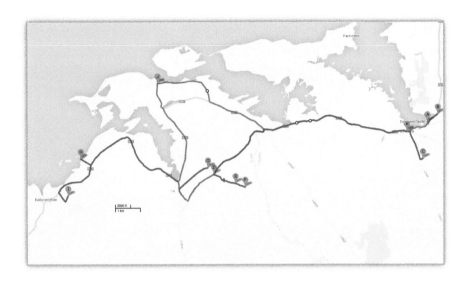

KINVARA TRAIL:

TOTAL DISTANCE 👉 49.7 km

AUDIO FILE:

http://www.earthwise.me/product/burren-trails-audio/

Kinvara 53.138816, -008.937276

Kinvara's picturesque harbour hosts the also picturesque Dun Guaire Castle built in 1520, close to where King Guaire in the seventh century had his main base. It is said that such was the generosity of King Guaire that his right arm grew longer than his left through giving so readily! He granted land to his kinsman St Colman, son of Duagh, so he could build a monastery. You can visit this on Gort Trail 1. Colman's Kilmacduagh features the tallest round tower in Ireland and is not to be missed! (King Guaire also held a castle in Gort town–this has long disappeared on a small island in the neglected river that runs through the town.)

POINT A: DUN GUAIRE CASTLE KINVARA 53.1458, -008.92566   1 km

DUN GUAIRE CASTLE

Start your tour by walking along the harbour wall to the 16th century castle, built by the O'Hynes clan who rose to power in later centuries. With sea defences on three sides, this was an ideal location for a castle in unstable times. After periods of hard rainfall, look and listen out for the underground streams that tumble into the bay in several places here. If the tide is out you might sight these springs. The water comes from many rivers in the Gort Lowlands where the oldest rocks in the Burren are found. Some of these streams will have passed through a turlough we encounter at Point C.

In the days when fishing was still a vibrant industry in Kinvara, the fishermen would pull alongside these springs to draw fresh water for brewing their tea. They knew exactly where to halt their hookers ("hookers" here refers the local style of fishing boats which were designed with distinct hooked ends- hence the name 'hookers"!). Local folk also told me that eels used to swim the underground rivers for many miles before emerging at the sea here! An ancient fortification can be seen in ruins on a small headland in the bay as you walk toward the castle. King Guaire's original castle was quite a sophisticated wooden structure, protected by a moat that also held a fish pond. It was well fortified and known as the Fort of the White Sheeting. In its heyday bards would come from afar to recite their poetry at this popular venue. You may wish to visit the more modern Dun Guaire castle. *There is a car park on your right.*

RESUME WHEN READY

After passing the castle to your left on the main road, stop just past the first turning on your left hand side.

POINT B: ST COLMAN'S WELL/TOBER MAC DUAGH
53.14471, -008.92043   550 m

You will see an old stone cross in the field and a tree adorned with rags flagging the side road, close to a stile into the field. This beautiful well was discovered quite recently under a large spread of brambles! No doubt Tobar Mac Duagh Well was in use in the days when the original castle was inhabited. It would be marvellous if the castle was likewise rescued from the wilderness that has smothered it. Like the original castle, the well had succumbed to ruination. Many of these wells remained holy spots to which people would come to pray, often walking around them in silent prayer while they literally relinquished their worries to the healing waters.

RESUME WHEN READY

OF TOBER MAC DUAGH

RAGGY TREE BY WELL

Go back to Kinvara and take the first left that takes you past the post office, also on your left. Shortly after where the road divides, take the right hand fork. Drive on for about 2km and look out for the brightly coloured signs for Burren Nature Sanctuary. Turn left and follow the short road round to the car park.

POINT C: BURREN NATURE SANCTUARY 53.12946, -8.92736   2.6 km

There is an extensive playground, nature walks and other features here. We are going to visit the turlough mentioned at Point A. A turlough is a lake that disappears and reappears according to rainfall levels, and is a distinct feature of limestone scenery in the Burren. Without a doubt the rapid changes wrought by turloughs coming and going adds a magical value to the landscape of the Burren.

Fifty millions years the senior of the Burren uplands, the landscape around here has worn down to gentle undulating plains in which the rivers dip and rise, creating disappearing lakes, or turloughs in their wake. There are numerous turloughs in this region. This one at the Sanctuary has fluctuating water levels that are in part due to its close proximity to the sea. It is affected by both rainfall and the tide! The trees that encase this turlough lend it a particularly alluring atmosphere.

To reach the turlough follow the signpost for the turlough and take the path that leads behind the main building. The path leads to the right hand side of the building and then across the field and down a grassy avenue before it reaches the turlough with a viewing platform.

PHOTO K4: SEAT OVERLOOKING TURLOUGH AFTER HEAVY RAINFALL

This turlough is a small one but some can be wide and stretch for miles, such as Lough Bunny on Gort Trail 1. Despite its small size the turlough here performs quite a task for the underground river system. It is here that at least three rivers emerge from nearby Kiltartan, some kilometres away to the south east. The rivers filter out through swallow holes in the bottom of this turlough and make their way to sea in Kinvara Bay. The coming and going of the turloughs create specialized plants and a certain ambience unique to this area of Ireland.

The other nature walk at the sanctuary is also quite enchanting as it takes you along winding paths in typical Burren limestone scenery, incorporating a deserted small settlement en route! There are even some fairy houses created for everyone's delight. At the end of the visit enjoy a wholesome early lunch in their pleasant cafe facing a water garden. Their food produce is sourced locally.

RESUME WHEN READY.

Return to Kinvara and turn left. Follow the N67 continuing south towards Ballyvaughan. After 7km you reach the first major junction, where two roads join from the left. You will see a Welcome to County Clare sign just past this junction. Take the road on the left signposted L1014 CARRAN. After about 3 kilometres you pass a thriving chocolatier on the left hand side. Park at the start of the next small road on the left.

POINT D: PARKING SPOT FOR WALK TO OUGHTMAMA 53.12065, -009.05108   10 km

Walk up the stony lane. Further up the lane will veer to the left and then wind back round. Keep walking uphill on the track, with the valley on your right and the slopes on your left. After about ten minutes walking, glance into the fields to your right and you should be able to see the gable ends of some ruined churches. You can enter into the fields through gates provided but make sure not to enter if animals are in the fields. The best way in is from further up the track, where you can double back a little.

POINT E: walk from track across fields to Oughtmama
             (1.1km as far as this point)

This ecclesiastical settlement is Oughtmama, named after the area, meaning "The Breasted Hill". The churches are believed to be from the twelfth century, and legend has it that there were originally seven churches there. You may wish to visit the holy well first which is situated at the end of the track and up the slopes to the left.

To reach the well walk to the end of the path where you will see a gate ahead. Follow the wall to the left of the gate as it leads gently uphill. When that wall peters out and bushes line up from the right look upwards to the left ahead and you will see a lone ash tree bending sharply to the right. This is protecting St Colman's Well. Sacred trees often accompanied holy wells, though many have been lost over time. Most of the wells in this region are named after St Colman. It is said that he had an earlier church in Oughtmama where the church ruins lie. Some believe it is another Colman who later lived at nearby Corcomroe Abbey.

RESUME WHEN READY

POINT F: ST COLMAN'S WELL   (400m along track)

ST COLMAN'S WELL
ABOVE OUGHTMAMA

The well is a place of inward reverie. Renowned for healing eye afflictions, St Colman's Well is adorned with holy ornaments and other objects that visitors deposit. . If you look down the slope you should be able to see quite clearly the churches – as I said, only three remain of the legendary seven churches of Oughtmama. Walk down toward the churches if you did not visit them earlier. Depending on the weather conditions you may spot a trickle of water flowing downhill towards the churches. There was a mill race and mill near the churches, as this was a monastic site too–you can see the water running above ground a bit more near the site remains of the mill, situated beyond the churches. There was enough water flowing naturally for it to enter a horizontal mill wheel and turn the paddles in the lower storey of a wooden mill, long disappeared. Grain would have been placed in the upper storey where the millstone was connected to a stationary millstone beneath it. The upper millstone turned and ground the corn beneath. The early Cistercian monastery here may well have relocated to Corcomroe later. The Cistercians were skilled farmers and water engineers. Here the monks cultivated a stripped field system. It might be hard to spot both the enclosures and the field systems but if you stand on Turlough Hill above and look north across this hidden valley you can see them more easily.

As in England, the Cistercians enclosed their churches in an east-west line–their inner enclosure is about one hundred metres wide and is still visible in part. There were other buildings too in this 20 metre enclosure. The leacht or preaching mound opposite the west end of the innermost churches is worth noting. One of the churches lies in the outer enclosure only and is orientated more north easterly.

A northeast orientation is common in very sacred places such as Stonehenge and Chartres Cathedral. It often signifies that the priests were aware of higher knowledge when they orientated the church this way, since mystics regard the north east as the entry direction for the highest spiritual programmes. On the water stoup in the larger church are some intriguing dragon-like creatures carved with intertwining necks.

Again this is an indicator of initiatory knowledge being used, for dragons often reference a strong telluric (of the earth) force. Indeed there is a major ley line extension of the pentagram grid drawn by Tony Peart that aligns with the position of these churches. This ley also links with St Colman's Hermitage below Eagle's Rock! Given that the early monks walked these leys and created their oratories on them, the noted alignment strengthens the case for St Colman having been here.

If you then start to climb uphill to the right of the well you can follow walls leading up Turlough Hill, which is to your right—you could also enquire about visiting this hill with a local guide who can be contacted at the chocolatier. Many wild goats roam this terrain and are enjoyable to watch. Leave yourself three full hours for the walk and the ascent and descent of the hill, and be sure to take an OS map with you. **Only venture up Turlough Hill alone on a clear day, as the weather can change quite rapidly when cloud cover comes in.**

TURLOUGH HILL

After about half an hour you reach a rare type of enclosure marked on the map. This stone enclosure covers a wide area and has deliberate gaps often marking the cardinal directions, two of which align with large cairns on neighbouring hilltops.

Turlough Hill is the most suggestive ritual landscape in the Burren, probably used in Neolithic times. The enclosure is at the eastern end of Turlough hill, so you will encounter it first if climbing from St Colman's Cave. It's typical of what are known as causewayed enclosures of the Neolithic period in Britain. Since there is a severe lack of soil here to create a deep trench, they laid their hands on what was plentiful: stones. With its upright stones and well defined gaps in cardinal directions that indicate causeway routes into the enclosure, there is a definite possibility the site was created for ceremonial purposes. It certainly does not make sense as a normal defensive fort, for these were built in a far later period. It would be very good if someone studied this enigmatic site to consider possible alignments with the movements of the stars and Sun and moon, particularly since other large cairns line up with it. There may be a lunar standstill involved at midsummer for instance, or an alignment with the setting of the sun at some time of year. Aubrey Burl in the UK was a foremost researcher into the relatively new field of archaeo-astronomy. Academics are starting to take the research more seriously.

Note there is a giant cairn outside the circular enclosure at the western end, surrounded by about 80 hut circles–so obviously people gathered there in greater numbers than would have been able to support themselves there all year long. There would have been between 6 and 8 people staying in each hut, so we are looking at a minimum of 500 people gathering on this hill for some sort of seasonal celebration. The cairn is at the western end of the hill, and most appropriately the west was associated with death. The ceremonial enclosure is at the eastern end, and the east was associated with initiation. Being situated on the easternmost hill, overlooking the Burren Lowlands, it has been suggested that the site was ideally suited for large groups of people to arrive from both the Burren Uplands and the Burren Lowlands. Archaeologists view it as a "liminal place". This means it represents a threshold, not just geographically but spiritually too. Landscapes that reflected and conjured up inner states were used for ceremonial purposes in ancient times.

By way of further musing, the valley in which the Oughtmama churches were placed exudes a sense of peace and other-worldiness. It was associated with three St Colmans, and Colman was the local saint in the seventh century par excellence. Since there were seven churches at Oughmama in the folk memory of the land, it makes me wonder if there is an astronomical link here too. Could the seven sister stars of the Pleiades be represented here? Both the number 7 and that constellation are associated with the divine feminine and also in current times to a shift taking place in consciousness worldwide. Certainly this valley is linked to strong female energies and its name in Irish reflects this–it means "Breast of the pass" referring perhaps to the two hill tops on Turlough Hill and the valley below in which the churches are situated. With the church unusually orientated to the north east it may be that the valley and hill have both been used more than once as a sacred and ceremonial landscape.

RESUME WHEN READY

Return to your car/bike and continue on the road towards Carron by turning left onto the main road from the track you walked down. After about 2km you can pause and look back on the right hand side across the fields to view a lovely setting of our next stop Corcomroe Abbey, with Abbey Hill behind it. You will realize then why this monastery was also known as St Mary of the Fertile Rock, for there are many rich green fields surrounding the abbey. The Cistercians used the most advanced farming methods in their day and would have applied their knowledge to this rocky place. (See front cover for alternative view of Corcomroe.)

Take an acute right turn when you reach the first junction on the right. There are many signposts there, including a brown tourist sign for Corcomroe Abbey. Shortly you will pass some holiday homes on your right before taking a small cul-de-sac to the right discreetly signposted for Corcomroe Abbey. Drive the short distance and park at the end.

POINT G: CORCOMROE ABBEY 53.12648, -009.05447   3.5 km

COWS AT
CORCOMROE

The Cistercian abbey was founded in the late twelfth century—the churches extant at Oughtmama date from the early eleventh to the late twelfth century coincidentally, and it has been said that the Cistercians may have been briefly at Oughmama. However experts think that its founder Donal O'Brien, son of the King of Munster and King of Thomond, brought monks there in 1195 from Inishlouhaght (meaning Island of the Fresh Milk) on the banks of the river Suir in Tipperary. Traditionally the O'Connors were the leading family here. They controlled the barony of Corcomroe. Building of the current abbey started in the thirteenth century. By the fifteenth century it already was too poor a community to support a full contingent, so they built a crude dividing wall in the abbey to shrink the church size. Overall the abbey shows many signs of poor design abilities, in terms of both alignments and measurements. It by no means matches the architectural wonders of contemporary Europe. However, despite the inattention to detail you can sense great tranquillity in the wonderful setting. The best masonry lies in the eastern end where you can see lilies of the valley and poppies carved among the heads in the choir area. The reclining figure is Conor na Siudaine O'Brien, one of the monastery's main benefactors. He was the grandson of the founder. A wider cluster of buildings has mainly disappeared or gone into serious decay. For instance, there was a gatehouse just before where the car park starts today. Its arch fell in 1840. The building to the right hand side of the car park was probably an infirmary, and the abbot's house is covered in briars behind the church in another field. Overtaken often by Mother Nature, how fitting that the late poet and philosopher John O'Donohue said Mass on Easter sunrise here, since his work was so inspired by nature.

RESUME WHEN READY

BELL HARBOUR AT DAWN

Turn right onto the main road at the end of the lane, taking care as this is a blind spot. Just before the pub on your right there is a community defibrillator. Just ahead of you lies a bay called Bell Harbour.

This is a lovely inlet to stop and reflect at. Excavations of food dumps called middens at Corcomroe revealed evidence of a high seafood consumption rate. Bell Harbour is rich in seafood, and also the local seaweed would have been used to make compost in the monastic gardens.

At the main junction take a left on the main N67 to drive the coast road in the direction of Ballyvaughan. After about 5 kilo-

metres you come to a road on the right hand side leading to the sea, with signposts either side to Bishop Quarter. Turn down this cul de sac to explore a stretch of natural coastline with sand dunes and a lagoon. If you pass a ruined medieval church high on the left hand side you have gone too far on the main road and need to turn back.

POINT H: BISHOP QUARTER 50.126544, -009.05430   6.8 km

There are lovely views towards Black Head to the left and the Martello tower on the peninsular to your right.

SAND DUNES

RESUME WHEN READY

Return to the main road and turn right. Drive on for a couple of kilometres and take the turning signposted L5036 to the left. Take the first turning on the left again to reach Lough Rask. Near the end there is a small lay-by outside a house on the right, or choose to park on the grass near the stile at the end of the lane. Walk over the stile and down the lane to Lough Rask.

POINT I: LOUGH RASK 53.12973, -009.12902   3 km

SWAN ON LOUGH RASK

A local writer Ré O Laighléis has written Battle for the Burren, a lovely imaginary tale based on actual warring clans that existed here in 1317. The hag of Lough Rask appeared to one of the armies who were en route to Corcomroe. Donogh

O'Brien did not heed her warning though! The lake has a lovely trail round it through pleasant native woodland, offering views of wild swans and other water birds – this a place for binoculars, if you have them, to scour the lake and hillside for wildlife.

RESUME WHEN READY

Now return in the direction of Kinvara, by turning right at the end of the road to rejoin the main coast road. Instead of turning inland at Bell Harbour, which took you round Corcomroe as before, keep straight on the coast road. When you see a sign-post for the Russell Art Gallery turn left on the L5124, and then turn almost immediately right, following the signs for Russell Art Gallery.

You are now moving onto the Finvarra peninsula. Two Martello towers are visible on the horizon. These were defence towers built to defend against possible French invaders during the Napoleonic War. Forty men could live on the first floor above the gunpowder that was kept on the ground floor. There was a water tank then in the basement. Since Galway Bay offers sheltered harbours and safe landing spots, the area had to be protected. By placing the towers strategically at the tips of these peninsulas men were able to fire on any landing place and have a good vista too. Three Martello towers were built in total in the bay.

MARTELLO TOWER ON COASTLINE

POINT J: NEWQUAY 53.15535, -009.08051 11.4 km

When you reach the Art Gallery which is well signposted, you have the opportunity to take a lovely circular walk known as the Flaggy Shore. Lady Gregory and Yeats used to enjoy breaks at Mount Vernon House there, facing the sea. This is a lovely villa built in 1798 for Colonel William Persse, an ascendant of Lady Gregory, the great reviver of Irish arts in the late nineteenth century. Persse had been in the American War of Independence and had become friends with the first American President George Washington who had entertained him at Mount Vernon, his home in Fairfax, Virginia. Hence Persse chose this name for his holiday home.

To start the circular walk, turn left at the art gallery and then right immediately, so you are in effect going straight ahead at the Gallery using a staggered junction. The road swings round to the left past the beach and then later runs parallel with the Flaggy Shore, a pleasant expanse of flat rock you can walk on beside the sea. The sea road swings left past a lovely lake, at the end of which you turn left to pass by the ruins of the Skerrit's large house on the right before coming to a triangular-shaped garden at a junction. Carry straight on by staying to the left side of the garden and later you will find yourself back at the gallery. The walk is about 6km long. *Continue on a short distance to reach the renowned fish pub-restaurant Linnanes, on the left hand side in Newquay.* On a fine day you can sit out and, if lucky, watch the fisherman unload their lobster pots here in the small harbour.

RESUME WHEN READY

Finally head back to Kinvara by driving on alongside the sea until you reach the main coast road, where you turn left.

Kinvara   10.8 km

END OF KINVARA TRAIL

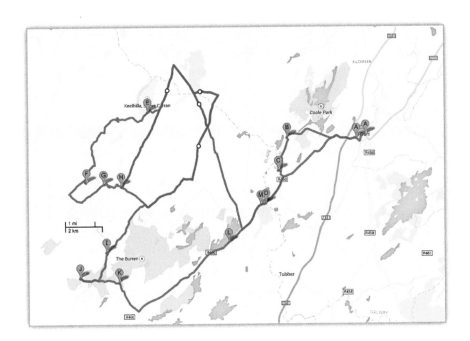

GORT TRAIL 1:

TOTAL DISTANCE ☞ 61.4 km

AUDIO FILE:

http://www.earthwise.me/product/burren-trails-audio/

POINT A: GORT 53.06406, -008.82257

Gort began as an unimpressive town in the middle of the eighteenth century. However, in the seventh century there was a widely-known chieftain living here – King Guaire, who became King of Connacht (one of Ireland's main four provinces) in around 655. He was related to St Colman who was noted for his saintliness in the area. King Guaire, who also lived at Dun Guaire Castle in Kinvara, was so generous it is said that one of his arms grew longer from giving alms! He also was a generous host, and there is record of one distinguished party of over 300 guests staying for a year and a month when Ireland's chief poet Seanchan Torpest brought his colleagues and pupils with him. The Shaughnessy clan were the local chieftains until the end of the seventeenth century. They lost their land to the Prenderghasts, whose descendant Thomas Prenderghast in the early nineteenth century vastly improved the look and layout of the town. In current times the town still has some good buildings from the latter half of the nineteenth century, but it has suffered more than most towns in the west from the collapse of the economy in the early part of the twenty first century. Having said that, it serves as a popular market town and hosts a large community of Brazilians who came to work in a meat factory during the boom years! It also is in my view a very tolerant place to live, and is an excellent gateway to the Burren.

STARTING POINT *Leave Gort by the Kinvara/Corofin road which starts opposite Supervalu further down the wide street the main church is on. It is the main right hand turn as you come from the square. After you pass over the motorway turn right to Kinvara. Note the turlough to your right.* This is Coole Turlough that so captured the imagination of poets such as WB Yeats who composed the poem The Wild Swans, while gazing out on it.

Soon you come to the end of the turlough or disappearing lake and reach a junction with the road signposted to Kinvara to the right. Drive past this junction and stop by the church.

STAINED GLASS WINDOW
AT TIERNEENAN

You may collect a key to this church from the adjoining bungalow. When you enter the church you will be facing a stained glass window. Look carefully for a fly, a cock, flying dishes and a girdle on his garment. These all feature in the story of St Colman's miraculous life. Above the altar the main window features a very tall round tower you will encounter on your next stop.

RESUME WHEN READY

Continue on the road you were driving. The road goes past a turning for Gort Golf Club on the left and then a small school on the right. After winding on for a few minutes you come upon a

series of stone buildings amidst a large cemetery. The large car
park is on the right at the start of these monastic ruins.

POINT C: KILMACDUAGH 53.04931, -008.88741   2.2 km

ROUND TOWER AT KILMACDUAGH

This is Kilmacduagh, Church of the son of Duagh, one of the most important ecclesiastical centres in Ireland in medieval times. You can collect a bunch of keys from the bungalow opposite to enter the main cathedral, the old churches and the tower house. The buildings date from the ninth to the fourteenth century and an explanatory diagram is displayed outside the car park. With key in hand first walk down a narrow lane by the notice board outside the car park. It runs down to the thirteenth century O'Heynes Abbey. At the end of a long straight section, a stile leads you into the cloister foundations. Built over St Colman's Monastery, this church has details remaining of Romanesque carvings above the capitals in the chancel. The stone masons here were of high calibre. Some of the buildings to the south are blocked off– if you walk round to the east side of them and perch on a loose boulder lying nearby, you can peep inside the far window and make out some stone effigies, possibly of past bishops or other ecclesiastical figureheads. It is believed that the treasury lay within this section of the building too. The grassy area at the south end of the building has strong telluric energies: the earth energies create a vortex here, and it feels very positive to stand there. From this sheltered spot you can look out towards the tall round tower that stands amidst the gravestones. This is Ireland's tallest round tower extant – it stands at over 111 feet, and its main door is 26 feet above the ground. There is rubble infilling to a certain level, as often is the case with these enigmatic towers, whose purpose people are divided over. In my book Spirit of the Burren I devote an entire chapter to the various functions that these towers perform, in particular highlighting the work of entomologist Professor Calahan, who presents a convincing case for the towers creating local hot spots of fertility, in which the monks would grow herbs, high-yielding crops and other produce.

You are more than welcome to book some time with me to explore this site, and learn how to dowse or divine, including how to dowse the aura around the round tower. We can also dowse a pattern of ley lines that connect the various buildings from different centuries with one another. My email is jackiequeally@gmail.com

This sprawling monastic complex was founded in the seventh century by St Colman when he walked from his cave retreat that we shall visit later on this trail. His cousin King Guaire had promised him land upon which to build a monastery. Colman walked via a series of local wells, which in later centuries attracted pilgrims who left rosary beads and small crosses when visiting. Some of the extant wells are on private land and so are not accessible, but we shall see the penultimate one on our next stop. The final well on his journey was close to the monastery but has disappeared under modern farming practices. Colman knew that there would be a sign of where to stop and build his new spiritual home. He was divinely guided to create his monastery when his knotted girdle fell suddenly to the ground. This occurred at Kilmacduagh in 610 CE. His church was wooden and is long gone. St Colman himself is said to be buried in Colman's Bed where the tightly packed yews shroud a more modern bishop's grave, close by the door to the cathedral. Colman inspired other monks to create similar settlements long gone. We know there was a St Folia and her brother St Colgan for instance. Under Colman's influence the entire area round Gort hosted many wooden churches, replaced later with stone ones, most of which have fallen into decay and oblivion. In 625 Colman retired to the quiet hidden valley of Oughtmama visited on the Kinvara trail. This was the valley of the seven churches of which only three stone examples remain.

I get the distinct impression that Colman was a geomancer, knowing the ancient art of placement according to telluric forces. St Brendan of Birr and St Columba were also gifted in this regard. Churches are often built on sites that are sacred in their own rights due to the forces of subtle harmonious energy inherent in the land.

In a more romantic vein, Ireland's foremost architect of the time built Kilmacduagh. The 'Gobhan Saor' had been miraculously blessed with the art of architecture and stone masonry by St Madoc of Ferns Abbey in southeast Ireland. King Guaire had spent time at Ferns, and so invited the mason to oversee the building of his monastery. The oldest extant churches are St John the Baptist in the field outside the cemetery, and possibly St Mary's across the road, although it was rebuilt at some stage. In St Mary's there is a fantastic stone in the corner inside with St Andrew crosses in the corners. These tiny churches may well be as early as the ninth century. Others have disappeared. The Cathedral's oldest part is in the west where a low door with large overhead lintel has been infilled. This end of the cathedral would probably date from the 12th century. The aisles off the main nave belong to local families of import. For instance the Shaughnessys, the then chiefs of the area round Gort, were appointed custodians of Colman's crozier, part of which is preserved in the National Museum of Ireland. Inside the entrance to their aisle on the right is a face that almost looks as if it is straight out of a modern cartoon. The face has large ears with dangling lozenge type earrings! Note the remnants of some fine carvings in the high altar area.

If you walk to the back into the cemetery and look over the far back corner you will see an unusual square building whose origins archaeologists are unsure of. Situated overlooking the marshes and turlough, this was probably an early ecclesiastical building, possibly for administrative purposes. Again when dowsing it there are some interesting patterns of earth energies I can discern.

As you walk back towards the car park, take the key and open the door to the square tower. Inside there are two more floors overlooking what would have been the main part of the house. The building was possibly a bishop's residence. Note the alcove projecting north with side chamber–this is thought to have been a preaching pulpit or oriel, from which the bishops would bless the many pilgrims who came from the mid 14th century onward. This building might well have served as a seminary also.

Kilmacduagh lasted until the end of the seventeenth century when England introduced the Penal Laws which brought about the demise of this 1100 year old monastery. Largely forgotten, it was the equal of Clonmacnoise on the Shannon in its heyday.

RESUME WHEN READY

Return to the car park and leave by turning right. The road weaves its way round the monastic complex which now hosts the main cemetery for the local town of Gort. At the junction with the Gort-Corofin road turn right towards Corofin. After a couple of miles on the right there is a gap in the hedgerow, revealing steps down to the final well extant that St Colman would have stopped at en route to founding his monastery. You know you have gone too far if you see a small public car park marking the entrance to some public woodland on the left. *To visit the well you can park here or outside a smart bungalow a little further back on the left.*

COLMANS WELL, COROFIN ROAD

It is fun to dowse with divining rods at the holy wells. Often you can find both ley lines and water lines at such sites, and it is this criss-cross of lines that mark out a holy well. The waters at many wells in the area were regarded as healing and sacred. A group of farmers in the Beagh district have tidied up, and in general made their wells more attractive. This well was one which they treated thus.

Now we will explore where St Colman lived before he became abbot of Kilmacduagh. This involves a journey into the limestone hills of the Burren.

RESUME WHEN READY

Continue on the road and soon you will see on the left a large sign for Clare FM Radio 96.4, a pleasant local radio station. In the lay-by beside it there is a display for Bunakippaun Woodland Attyslany, which as a government-owned nature reserve won an award for its promotion of deciduous woods. *Travel on towards Corofin as far as the first crossroads, where the crossroads indicate Corofin ahead, Tubber to the left and Ballyvaughan 29km to the right. Turn right. Travel about 10 km until you reach a crossroads with Kinvara to the right and the Burren Perfumery marked to the left. Turn left and take the right hand fork in the road later, which is a very twisty winding road leading toward the limestone cliffs. Stop when you reach an opening on the right for cars to park.* There is a large informational board in the car park. There is another interpretative board at the entrance to the walk on the right. The panels inform you about the geology and flora of the Burren National Park to which this land belongs

POINT E: KEELHILLA PHOTO 53.07629, 008.99898   14.8 km

This is a fascinating, well-demarcated walk that follows in part an old medieval pilgrim path. When I first discovered this hideaway spot below the cliffs there was no path leading up to it, and I must admit it was much more of a thrill to first hear about it and then search for it among the thick hazel scrub. You can get a sense of this if you deviate from the track laid down by volunteers. You can wander later through moss-laden tunnels in the dense hazel woods and find unexpected clearings where fairies are bound to dwell! For now continue on the path as it leads you over limestone pavement with its clints and grykes, in which many stunted trees and bushes grow. If you look down a particularly deep gryke, or groove, you get a sense of the abundant insect and plant life that exists, hidden from view of most passers-by, who hurry on to view the hidden retreat where St Colman lived his early years as a hermetic. The story goes that when the King of Connacht heard that the unborn Colman of the royal ancient Dathai family was to become the most famed member of all the high ranking families, he grew so jealous he ordered his death. This entailed murdering his pregnant mother Rhinagh. There followed a series of miraculous events in which the pregnant woman survived all attempts on her precious life. And so it was that Colman was born and then baptized in secret, with water that miraculously emerged from under a tree during the rite. Colman was reared by monks, and when old enough he went to Inismor, the island of utmost sanctity in the Aran Isles. Leaving behind two churches there in his name, Colman retreated into the Burren hills with one companion monk. In a small cave on *Cinn Aille,* a dramatic limestone escarpment beneath Eagle's Rock, the two men devoted themselves to meditation and the spiritual life.

HERMITAGE CAVE

The mouse, fly and cock became Colman's constant companions for seven years, and are commemorated in the stained glass window you saw in Tierneevin Church (see Point A). One Easter morning, following an intense period of fasting, the second unnamed monk complained of hunger. Taking pity on him, Colman prayed for sustenance. Almost immediately the entire contents of a banquet being held in Dunguaire Castle took off through the air and literally flew towards the cave. By now the local king was none other than Colman's cousin, and he was a far kinder man than the predecessor who had ordered his mother's murder. King Guaire ordered his guards to ride out and follow the dishes. The guests followed behind, and all were astonished to find the monks feasting on their banquet where it had landed on the rocks, close to their wooden oratory and cave. It is also said that the horses' hooves stuck fast in the rock and could not move until Colman had had his fill and raised his hand to free them! When the news reached him King Guaire marvelled at his long lost cousin's powers, delighted to realise he was still alive! He granted Colman freedom to roam until he found the site he favoured to build a monastery on, and the rest is history–apart from the fact that the companion monk had died of over-consumption from eating too quickly. His stone burial grave can be seen on the far side of the long wall on the limestone pavement beside what seems to be a leacht, or preaching base. It could be that the supposed grave is in fact a dry well and the other pile of stones is his resting place. The footprints and dish marks in the flat rocks can be reached by walking further along a small path beside the long wall as you walk away from the car park. Follow the long wall parallel to the cliffs and then climb through a stile onto the 'Bothar na Mias' (Field of the dishes).

WELL BESIDE SAINT'S GRAVE?

RESUME WHEN READY

From the car park, carry on the same road. It leads you in about 7 km to an interesting port of call: a perfumery! Their drive is to the left with a sign on the roadside. If you miss it, reach the end of the road and retrace yourself for about 1.5 km.

POINT F: BURREN PERFUMERY 53.04519, -009.04830   7.1 km

Apart from a delightful garden, there is a film and gift shop and pleasant cafe where you can take lunch.

RESUME WHEN READY

Drive back to the road and turn left to reach the end of the road where you turn left again. The road climbs up steeply and takes you to a wonderful viewpoint over the Burren mountains with plaques to highlight topography.

POINT G: VIEWPOINT 53.04276, -009.02919   3.6 km

RESUME WHEN READY

Then continue through Fahee and at the bottom of the hill you will see a small road to the left signposted 12km to Kinvara, almost opposite a bungalow. You now are in the valley of Glencolumkille. Park outside the walls of the white bungalow, opposite the road sign, and walk up the road to the left. First pass a farm gate on the right, and then walk up a small lane on the left. Wear waterproof boots as this lane is often water-logged. It leads you to an enchanting basin area fed by local springs. The water gathers in a structure known as St Columba's Well.

POINT H: GLENCOLUMKILLE WELL 53.04163, -009.01730   5.2 km

ST COLOMBA'S EYE WELL

FULUCHT FIA BESIDE WELL

The well at Glencolumkille is called St Columba's Eye Well – many wells in the area are associated with healing eye afflictions. This is one of the few places associated with Columba/Columbkille who once visited the Aran Isles offshore from the Burren. A holy well in Fanore on the coast is dedicated to the same saint who is believed to be synonymous with Columba. I also found a very dilapidated church in his name nearby on private farmland. It is doubtful that this local saint Columbkille is the same as St Columba from Donegal in the far north, who went on to found the great monastery at Iona in Scotland. He may have been a local saint with the same name, as Columba the statesman lived a very busy life and left Ireland in a hurry.

Whoever lived here once, this inland well is still a marvellous place to meditate, beside the abundant streams. The simple stone cross is medieval and locals believe it once stood on top of the preaching cross up the hill. Your eye might be drawn to the trees growing on a mound to the fore of the springs—these are growing out of a fulucht fia, a mound of burnt stones that has been grassed over with time. When leaving the well walk back to the road you are parked on and walk a little further uphill to the left. There is a rock on the left hand side of the road bearing the finger marks of the saint, and on the right 50 meters away is the opening into the old church, which is quite possibly built on a more ancient sacred site. The base of the preaching cross near the gate contains a cavity said to be the repository for a missal.

RESUME WHEN READY

After 1.5 km on the same road, take the next turning to the right. This leads you past a world-famous icon with large gates and a driveway on the right–it was used in the opening sequence to each episode of Fr Ted's! Look out for it in view straight ahead on the right after 2.7 kilometres. (For a picture of it, see page 170)

POINT I: FR TED'S HOUSE 53.00971, -009.03010   4.3 km

You can only enter 'Craggy Island' upon prior arrangement for tea and cakes. The land this house stands on is rich in archaeological monuments. Near the house is an old church Tempail Patrick, a well, a "saint's bed" that has long disappeared and a holed stone through which children traditionally passed through to avoid catching rickets. The fort above the farm has connections with Lon the Smith, a three-legged mythical smith who dwelt in a cave with a cindered floor (see Ennis Trail)—there is a souterrain attached to the fort, though it is doubtful this was his home- often souterrains are mistaken for caves.

RESUME WHEN READY

Now carry on for 2.4 km until you reach a crossroads, which is within the Burren National Park. The following walk is an optional one which will take you at least two hours to complete. *If you turn up the 'green road' on your right, you can drive slowly up this rough track and park near the gate at the end of the road. Otherwise turn left at the crossroads to head into the National Park. (Gortlecka Crossroads is N52.99695 W009.03728)*

POINT J: LOUGH AVALLA PARKING SPOT   52.997519, -9.050411

2.7 km

HOLY WELL SCENE

ST PATRICK'S HILL AND LOUGH AVALLA

Walk into the left and follow the markers around Lough Avalla Farm, which is a demarcated farm walk offered by the farmer. It is not recommended to fit this in on a day's touring–it is something to return and do when you have enough time to enjoy it. It is a perfect place to forget time. The owners are dedicated to using organic and biodynamic methods in their farming, and their goats and cattle thrive on it. There is much to discover there, such as the delightfully lush watercress bed, set in the pure springs beside a holy well. This is marked off the road to the left, after ten minutes walking up the road towards their farm. If you have only a little time it is well worth visiting this peaceful spot. Across the stream are some fuluchta fia or burnt mounds–on the farm, the owner Harry Jeuken believes they are in fact foot saunas. On the walk you will encounter many goats, limestone cliffs, limestone pavement, magical woods and the small serene lake of Lough Avalla.

RESUME WHEN READY

After your walk return to the gate where you parked and retrace your route back to the start of the 'green road' by the crossroads. Cross straight over, where you continue along a hazel bordered proper road. Now you are back on the route shared by those who did not visit Lough Avalla Farm. Soon you will pass one of the Burren's main emblems as a marvellous vista opens out before you on the left.

You cannot miss the mountain of Mullaghmor,. It has the appearance of slightly runny jelly upturned from its mould! The jelly is really stepped limestone, liberally peppered with herbs and wild flowers that abound from May until September. 75% of all the plant species found in Ireland can be found in the Burren, as it has so many diverse habitats within a small region. 23 of the 27 species of orchid found in Ireland grow here too! Butterfly populations maintain good numbers and high species diversity here too. Bees also proliferate in this natural landscape. Wild goats would increase in number if they were not illegally culled from time to time.

POINT K: MULLAGHMORE IN BURREN NATIONAL PARK
52.99589, -009.021150   2 km

NORTHERN FLANKS OF MULLAGHMOR

Park on the wider verges close to where there are official path markers on the stone walls, and stretch your legs on a wonderful looped walk over Mullaghmore. Give yourself two hours to complete. Limestone can be a refreshing rock strata to walk on but the pavements can be very loose so do walk with care. The first marker is by a stile, as you approach from the crossroads at Gortlecka. The green arrow trail at the first lay-by is shorter–about 1.5 km long. Further along, the blue, red and green arrow trails, all of which are longer, are accessed over another stile and vary in length according to the panel.

RESUME WHEN READY

How was this scenery formed? I will attempt to explain. The limestone formed in more tropical conditions about 300 million years ago, over a period of about twenty million years when the sea covered this area. There were frequent Ice Ages that followed too. The limestone is oolitic, meaning there are egg-like pieces of limestone surrounded by fine sand–a result of the crushing of millions of sea creatures. Subsequent sea level changes helped create this strange-looking landscape by uplifting, dissolving and weathering the soft limestone into the karst landscape seen now. Bedding planes formed as the rocks formed during periods of long global upheaval. The buckling is due to massive earth movements when continents collided and the soft limestone hills were pushed up against one another. Horizontal breaks in the layers represent times when the limestone was exposed long enough to form thin soils, or shales, and chert (which is essentially the compacting of silica-rich shells of dead plankton from tropical seas). For the last 50-60 million years the rocks have been above sea level and have continued to weather and erode during rainfall. Then, in more recent Ice Ages, the rich deposits of sea mud were mainly carried away and large rocks called erratics were deposited. So the landscape is formed progressively by two processes; Karst processes and then glaciation. Underneath the Burren is a vast, relatively unexplored, territory of water, forming caves and rivers that are both wet and dry. I hope you can begin to understand why in recent years the Burren has been granted international geopark status.

RESUME WHEN READY

Continue on the road through the limestone scenery, passing a turlough or disappearing lake on your right. Fork left when a road joins from the right later. It takes you to the main road to Gort where you will turn left. When you pass a large lake on your left, pull into an open parking area on the edge of the shingle beach.

POINT L: LOUGH BUNNY 53.01371, -08.93247   8.6 km

LOUGH BUNNY

This is Lough Bunny, the most oligotrophic turlough in the Burren! When water is oligotrophic it means it is lacking in nutrients, and does not support large living creatures, since nutrients are low. However, it does allow adaptive plant species and creatures to thrive. The area around Lough Bunny is quite flat, as the rock is older and has been exposed to the elements longer. Rivers from the Slieve Aughties, hills a little inland to the east, carried away the protective layer of mudstones and shales, thus exposing the rock sooner to the weathering processes. Since the large lake is only a little above sea level and the depth is only 2 metres in most parts, the water has to be fed by springs. These lie along the shoreline parallel to the road. As you near the north end there are swallow holes along the shore that drain the water underground to meet with the waters of Coole Lough that you will encounter on the next Gort trail.

RESUME WHEN READY

Continue on the Gort road passing over the main crossroad where **you must stop and give way to traffic**. *Then after a couple of miles you should see an area of low woodland managed by Coilte on your right–park at the next bungalow on your right and walk on to the holy well across the road.*

POINT M/D: HOLY WELL, BEAGH 53.03383, -008.89947   3.3 km

This was POINT D you stopped off at earlier on the trail. You may like to wander down once more and reflect on all that you have heard and seen of this magical area!

RESUME WHEN READY

Continue onto Gort.

Gort 53.06406, -008.82257   4.5 km

END OF GORT TRAIL 1

GORT TRAIL 2:

TOTAL DISTANCE ☞ 45km

AUDIO FILE:

http://www.earthwise.me/product/burren-trails-audio/

POINT A: GORT

In the vicinity of Gort in the late nineteenth century, a substantial body of Anglo Irish resided. Some of these land-owners recognized how special the area was for folklore. They developed a remarkable interest in the Celtic twilight of fairy energies, and a certain element of mysticism. This aristocratic body became a highly influential movement, responsible for reviving native Irish identity throughout the arts. We begin this trail by visiting some of the ancient sites set within rural landscapes that would have inspired the storytellers of old. To reach a wonderful dolmen we have to skirt round the back of Lady Gregory's marital home. She lived at Coole Park with her husband, the well-travelled Sir William Henry Gregory, ex governor of Ceylon (now Sri Lanka). We shall hear more on him later. His second wife, the much younger Lady Augusta Gregory Persse, devoted herself to collecting fairy stories and folklore after he died of respiratory disease. She became a gracious hostess to many budding poets and writers of the day, including WB Yeats, so this trail is partly devoted to these refined revolutionaries who used the power of their pens rather than guns to influence the country.

Take the road opposite Supervalu (N53.06406° W008.82257°) out of Gort and travel over the motorway–take the first turning on the right towards Kinvara. Just before the parish church of Tierneevin comes into view on the right, take the very first turning right so you almost double back on yourself round the far side of the turlough (which beware in summer often disappears). There is a sign for Woodlands bed and breakfast on the corner at the start of this road. The road you are now on takes you around the back of Coole Lough, the large turlough on your right. *Drive on for two kilometres until you pass a car park on the right.* This is Garrylands that you can return to shortly. *Carry on until you reach a small humble crossroads and turn right down through farmland towards the woods in the near distance. Again, it will be signposted Woodlands B and B. At the end of this short road, turn left and go on a short distance. Either pull in near the bungalow on the left, or carry on to the right hand bend in the road and park on the outside bend* (GPS N53.10151° W008.86393°). A tall dolmen with leaning capstone should be visible in the distance on a rise beyond the turlough on the right (which might be dry depending on rainfall), on hazel scrub and limestone pavement. To access it, ask permission locally. Walk back toward the smart looking, double-storied farmhouse on the left, and go through the gate on the near side of it. This region was as high as the hills extant in the Burren once. Since this area round Gort is fifty million years older, the land is thus more eroded. It is known as the Gort Lowlands in official geological terms, and nowadays the area has become known as the Burren Lowlands. This term can remind people of its total connection with the Burren.

This walk is pleasant if there has not been too much rain. A kind local farmer told me that in the old days children used to have to walk to school across the turlough that forms in wet weather- so they brought their wellingtons with them and left them at the side of the turlough to change back into on the way home!

SECLUDED DOLMEN

This is a beautiful dolmen within stunning scenery. It seems that there is a large area of collapsed cairns immediately in front of the dolmen. Energetically, when I dowsed for telluric currents it was strong in some places among the stones. The main dolmen has a gentle energy, particularly inside it, and it is intimately connected to the stony area around it. I found that toning in the stony area could amplify the energies inside the dolmen, and then change the frequency of the immediate surroundings. There are some lovely places to sit in the woods behind and contemplate on the happy, peaceful atmosphere this place emanates.

RESUME WHEN READY

After walking back to the road, continue round the corner as the road veers to the left. Note the bungalow on the left, which appears after the farmhouse on the right. You may park just beyond the bungalow on the right. Walk back a little. Opposite the bungalow there is a low stone wall with a stile in it, usually well maintained. Go through this stile and pass through the nearby entrance gap to enjoy this splendid example of an old fort, often called a fairy fort.

POINT C: FORT AND WELL AT BALLYNASTAIG 53.10173, -008.86653

650 m

ANCIENT HOMESTEAD

Ballynastaig intriguingly means Town of the *Knitters* in Irish! Many times, when people talk of fairy forts in Ireland, they refer to charming small homesteads like this one. The ditch was defensive and protected some wooden homes long gone. You may see the remains of more recent stone homes that have collapsed here and there inside the rath, or fort. This rath, like some others in south Galway, also contains a souterrain – it is close to the exit in the ditch at the top left as you face away from the road. Crossing over that exit, you should notice some large flat stones on the ground concealing a hollow gap beneath. There is also an unusual large alcove in the ditch, and a fantastic well in the centre that has been preserved with steps and other features. There is a large recess at the back of the well too. This probably leads to the souterrain under the exit nearby.

When you walk out of the fort, look west toward the turlough in the near distance. There is a Norman ruined castle on the far side. This turlough is tidal and regularly receives waters from Kinvara Bay, which back up when the moon is affecting the tides. In other words, instead of the turlough freely draining via swallow holes, the ocean waters reach this lake via its underground streams. This is the best example of a tidal turlough in the Burren region. It is called Caherglassaun and one of Colmen's colleagues had a small oratory here on the edge of the lake—this is in quite a dilapidated state and not worth visiting.

RESUME WHEN READY

Carry on this small road past the fort and at the main road turn left and travel back as far as the car park on the left. This leads into Garrylands Woods, a nature reserve that form part of the Coole Turlough complex of disappearing lakes. This affords an excellent off-road walk.

POINT D: GARRYLANDS 053.07978, -008.87946   2.4 km

During dry periods you can walk or cycle right through to Coole Park, availing yourself of the conditions provided by the dry-bedded turlough, which in wetter weather will divide the woodlands. Thankfully some signposts and paths have been created to help guide you the 2.5 km through the dense woodland. Near the main entrance, to the right of the path, lies an old house that has been converted into a bat sanctuary! When in Coole Park stop by the old stable block for a good lunch. The stables were part of Lady Gregory's demense at Coole though the house was dismantled in 1941.

RESUME WHEN READY

To reach Coole Park, the next stop on our trail, continue on the road past the entrance to Garrylands and turn left at the T junction by the church at Tierneevin. This takes you onto the road you were on before. Turn left for Gort once you reach the main Gort-Corofin road. In Gort, if you wish to visit the Kiltartan Gregory Museum, a later stop on the same itinerary, turn right in the main square and call at the Sisters of Mercy convent beside the Bank of Ireland in the main street. Ask for Sister De Lourdes, who will happily oblige you with a tour if available. Otherwise, when you enter the square, turn left on your journey. At the main roundabout turn right onto the main Galway road, and after 1.7 kilometres the estate of Coole Park is signposted on your left. There is a fine lodge house on the far corner. Drive up this road and once you enter Coole Park you will be led through a lovely avenue of limes that lead to the car parks. Park in the sec-

ond car park which is nearer the stable block. There is a good free exhibition and film on the life of Lady Gregory at the small museum beyond the gates into the courtyard and cafe.

RESUME WHEN READY

POINT E: COOLE PARK FOR LUNCH 53.09229, -008.83700   9.7 km

OLD STEPS AT COOLE PARK

In Coole Park you can visit the walled garden, where the famous autograph tree grows in the open green area, close to the left hand path – it has a viewing platform built around it. This has many autographs recorded on it from visiting poets and writers who enjoyed Lady Augusta Gregory's hospitality. Together with WB Yeats who lived nearby, she was largely responsible for opening the Abbey Theatre in Dublin, Ireland's first live theatre which Irish writers like J.M. Synge would write plays for. If you retrace your steps from the walled garden back toward the exhibition centre, keep to the wide top path, passing the steps. On your right you pass the original foundations for Coole Park House which was dismantled by a local builder in the 1960s, following an accidental fire which had gutted the home. Turn right past a toilet block on your left and continue down to Coole Turlough that inspired Yeats to write the following poem:

The Wild Swans of Cole

'The trees are in their autumn beauty,
The woodland paths are dry,
Under the October twilight the water
Mirrors a still sky;
Upon the brimming water among the stones
Are nine-and-fifty swans.
The nineteenth autumn has come upon me
Since I first made my count;
I saw, before I had well finished,
All suddenly mount
And scatter wheeling in great broken rings
Upon their clamorous wings.
I have looked upon those brilliant creatures,
And now my heart is sore.
All's changed since I, hearing at twilight,
The first time on this shore,
The bell-beat of their wings above my head,
Trod with a lighter tread.

Unwearied still, lover by lover,
They paddle in the cold
Companionable streams or climb the air;
Their hearts have not grown old;
Passion or conquest, wander where they will,
Attend upon them still.
But now they drift on the still water,
Mysterious, beautiful;
Among what rushes will they build,
By what lake's edge or pool
Delight men's eyes when I awake some day
To find they have flown away?

RESUME WHEN READY

Leave the estate returning to the main road. Turn left and pass by a small primary school on the left. Take the next turning left, before a railway crossing. Across the road, at the start of the slip road over the railway, there is a brick building which was commissioned by Lady Gregory. You may note an old fashioned, somewhat exotic looking air, to this National School. Park away from the junction on the main side road that the church and belfry is on further along. Walk back to view the school.

KILTARTAN OLD SCHOOL:

As mentioned a while ago, this museum can be visited by arrangement with local historian Sr De Lourdes who resides in the convent besides the river in the main street in Gort.

As ex-governor of Ceylon Sir William Henry Gregory had agreed to donate a school to the neighbourhood when he retired to Coole Park. The school plans somehow were mixed up, and the Irish school was built in India while this fine oriental-looking one was built here! Sir William Henry Gregory lived from 1817 until 1892. He worked hard for land reform in Ireland. Inheriting quite a fortune from the East India Company he became a keen art collector, and briefly was a conservative MP before moving to Coole Park with his younger wife Augusta Persse, the daughter of a landowner near Kilchreest. The Persses were not popular landlords but Augusta was generous-hearted and deliberated to learn Irish. After her husband's death she propagated the revival of the language and Gaelic culture and wholeheartedly pursued her passions for a Celtic revival. She tapped into the rich tradition of folklore in south Galway and recorded it for posterity.

RESUME WHEN READY

Now drive a short distance up the side road until you see an old parish church low down on the left, with a more modern belfry beside it. Go into the car park on the right hand side opposite and walk into the modern cemetery on the outside of the old ruined church.

POINT G: KILTARTAN BURIAL GROUND 53.10087, -008.81899   300 m

You will see a grave with many flowers and ornamentations. This belongs to an highly skilled Polish diver who died tragically in recent years while mapping the vast system of underground rivers nearby. Close by and overlooking a deep cave where three underground rivers emerge, a sunken mausoleum stands. This is where Lord Gregory of Coole Park is buried, overlooking the cave where this tragic drowning occurred. To reach it, cross the road to the present Church of Kiltartan (the church down the steps). Go through the stile beside the church and walk straight across the field, away from the road. You may also access it via a gate beside the National School on the main Galway road. Beware of cattle and if there is a bull in the field, stay away.

GREGORY MAUSOLEUM

VIEW FROM MAUSOLEUM

RESUME WHEN READY

Leave the car park turning left and then left again onto the main road, in the direction of Galway. After a short distance you see a sign for Cummins Kitchens and Bathrooms on the right. Take the next small road on your right signposted on a brown tourist sign 'Thor Ballylee'. After about 2 km t*ake the very first road on the right. This is a very small road, poorly signposted "Thor Ballylee" on a small wooden post. The sign is often obscured with briars so take care. After a short distance you arrive at a large car park on the left hand side, where you can park.*

POINT G THOR BALLYLEE 53.10363, -008.77436   4.8 km

THOR BALLYLEE CLOSE UP

First walk up the road as far as the tower house in which Yeats lived between 1916 and 1929. It was a summer home and writer's retreat for Yeats, who had an insatiable appetite for mystical affairs, aided by his wife Georgina. Yeats changed the name Ballylee Castle to Thor Ballylee—"thor" being Irish for tower. The "tower symbolized the enchantment of rural Ireland. However, times became difficult as there was a lot of civil unrest following the Treaty of Independence. Here is a verse from one of the many poems he composed in his study in the tower. It reflects the turbulent times he lived in. Listen to it as you gaze at his tower.

Blessed be this place,
More blessed still this tower;
A bloody, arrogant power
Rose out of the race
Uttering, mastering it,
Rose like these walls from these
Storm-beaten cottages –
In mockery I have set
A powerful emblem up,
And sing it rhyme upon rhyme
In mockery of a time
Half-dead at the top.   Then look down at the water and contemplate:
An ancient bridge, and a more ancient tower,
A farmhouse that is sheltered by its wall,
An acre of stony ground,
Where the symbolic rose can break in flower
Old ragged elms, old thorns innumerable,
The sound of the rain or sound
Of every wind that blows;

The stilted water hen
Crossing stream again
Scared by the splashing of a dozen cows!

After looking at the race either side of the bridge, take a walk alongside the river on the car park-side of the bridge- it leads to an old mill and mill house. It is a very atmospheric place indeed and I can see why Yeats was inspired to write here.

RESUME WHEN READY

Now you may wish to end your tour by returning to Gort, or continuing beyond Gort to see some interesting natural phenomena. Either way, retrace your route to the main road by returning along the small road, turning left at the junction and then turning left onto the main road. Continue into Gort and pass right through the town. As you pass the extreme edge of town, you pass an 80km speed limit sign with a slipway on the left at a staggered crossroads. Take the right hand road past this and follow the road over the hump-backed bridge. Drive slowly where the road bends to the left. Stop at the farm gate on the left. Almost opposite there is a small track, which leads down to our next destination. Carefully walk by the wall on the left side. Soon you will notice the water below. Walk carefully in case the path is slippery and reach the edge of the river- notice that it comes out a cave under the road! This point is known as Caenahowan based on the meaning in Irish "head of the river" – it is a very deep cave. We now are going to trace where the river comes from before it emerges here and flows as the Gort river through town.

CAENAHOWAN

RESUME WHEN READY

Drive back to the start of the road and cross over the Ennis road by turning left toward Gort and then immediately right before the slipway on the right. You can park in this lay-by briefly to visit the grotto to Our Lady of Fatima facing the main road – if you peep over the wall there you will see the river disappearing under the road – it actually reappears briefly in a deep pool by the road we drove on just now, but we are going to visit the next point where the river disappears in a more dramatic style. *Continue up the byroad a short distance. On the left as the road rises there is a small lay-by large enough to accommodate 2 or 3 cars. Park here and climb over the style.*

Walk along the path and look to the right. You are facing into a collapsed river cave–the river has long disappeared underground. Walk further on and you will see a natural land bridge to the right with protective barbed wire on its edge–look down to the left over this and you overlook where the river actually disappears–leaving much debris and white foam in its wake. Return to the path and carry on further into an area of beautiful beeches with slopes sweeping down to the rushing river – you can go down here and explore the river bank for a while. You can also peer into the banks where the river disappears. As you return to the road along the path there is a smaller path leading to the right. This takes you to the next natural feature, known as the Churn – it is so called because at times of heavy rain the river swells and makes a churning noise. It is a very deep water hole protected by wire fencing. The river in this area keeps changing names as it ducks and dives its way along the Gort Lowlands, which are unmistakeably the oldest part of the Burren. Such features as we see here often occur locally. They also would occur totally underground in the Burren Hills to the south and west.

RESUME WHEN READY

Continue up the small road and take the next road to the left (it has a sign for Beagh Community Alert near the beginning of the road). This small road is very attractive but you have to be very careful driving, in the event of oncoming traffic. Keep left after seeing a bungalow on the right. Shortly, you will see the river on your left and a bench overlooking the river. Park at the second opening on the river where there is another bench directly facing the river.

POINT J: ST COLMAN'S WELL, BEAGH RIVER 53.05252, -008.79487

1.6 km

Turn to the left of the bench as you face the river and you can see a metal cross behind you near the river's edge. It is often submerged in the waters and marks St Colman's Well.

RESUME WHEN READY

St Colman's Well by river

POINT K: BEAGH OLD PARISH CHURCH 53.05252, -008.79487   300 m

Continue up the road and you will shortly arrive at some grand-looking iron gates on your left, before which you can park. Climb over the stile, or open the gates and walk through the leafy path. Further in lies a charming church that was in existence at least during the ninth century, when there are records of it being attacked by Vikings. These Vikings may well have visited nearby Kilmacduagh, as St John the Baptist Church was standing there then. Beagh Church may well have been on a pilgrim route to Holy Island in Lough Derg in East Clare, according to a local man Alan Johnston.

Beagh Church is the old parish church for this area, an area rich in wells, wedge tombs and forts. What is most odd about the ancient graveyard area is that there are two elongated fingers protruding out a long way from two corners of the irregular shaped graveyard. Also there is a definite sense of peace to the east of the church where some building once stood if you look at the ground carefully.

FINGER WALL AT OLD BEAGH PARISH CHURCH GRAVEYARD

RESUME WHEN READY

Now turn around and retrace your way to start of the road, and turn left at the junction. This area still retains the charm of old Ireland. Hares, deer and hen harriers still can be spotted. It is also no coincidence that there is a large estate nearby, for often estates become havens for wildlife to proliferate.

After one kilometre, on the left you pass a pathway with a yellow barrier into public woodland . This borders Lough Cutra Estate where Lord Gort, a Prenderghast who built the Georgian town of Gort, resided. Lough Cutra is named after one of the De Danaan princes in legendary times. He was a son of Umór and resided there. His brother Conall lived nearby at Kilbeacanty and one of his brothers was Aengus who founded the great fort Dún Aengus on the Isle of Inis Mor.

This estate has the largest privately owned lake in Ireland. I find it fascinating to see this lake on a map: it is shaped very much like the map of Ireland taken as a whole island! The private estate has spawned many local shooting clubs since introducing pheasants for commercial shooting parties. Just before reaching the main road regard its fine gates and the lodge house on the left.

POINT L: GATES OF LOUGH CUTRA ESTATE 50.03260, -008.81257

3.4 m

Turn right here for Gort.

Gort   53.06406, -008.82257   4.5 km

END OF GORT TRAIL 2

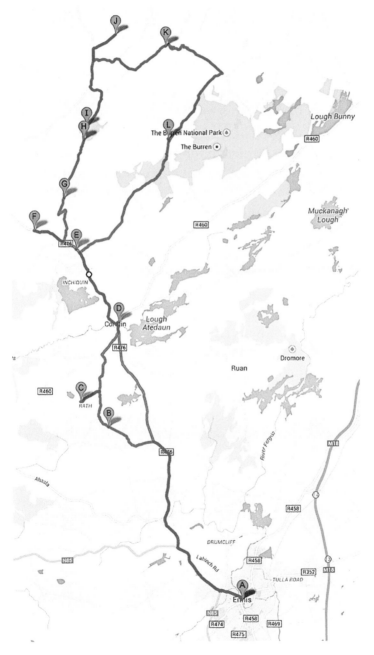

AUDIO FILE:

http://www.earthwise.me/product/burren-trails-audio/

POINT A: Ennis 52.846557, -8.986405

Leave the medieval market town of Ennis following the road for the N85 and Ennistymon, which leads off the roundabout beside the bridge over the river Fergus on the town's interior ring road. After about 2.5 km turn right onto the R476 which is signposted for Corofin. Look out for a turning on the left to Dysart O'Dea, which is about 4km along the road you are now on. To help you find it, after the turning signposted for Mauricemills on the left the road bends left and a sign for Corofin points towards a sharp bend to the right. Just before this bend, turn left onto the L4154. There is a sign for Corofin Text Alert Area at the right hand side of this road at the start. Once you turn down the road you have to travel for about 1.5km. Bear right at the fork in the road. (You may spot a quaint old tourist sign for Diseart Tola, Diseart O'Dea Church and Round Tower in the hedge growing on the left side at the start of the right hand fork.)

SIGNAGE FOR DYSART O'DEA:

Continue for about a kilometre and when you see a turnstile in the wall that leads into a graveyard on the right, park opposite in the lay-by. If it is full there is a gateway on the right past the church and graveyard. Park here at right angles to the road. Go through the turnstile....

POINT B: DYSART O'DEA CHURCH 52.908643, -9.068767   10.4 km

DOORWAY OF DYSART O'DEA CHURCH

This delightful site exudes a sweet feminine air. St Tola's well lies toward the right hand corner of the field as you enter from the roadside. The large house at the top of the field belongs to Patrick the farmer. If you see him ask his permission to walk across and visit the well. St Tola was a significant local saint in the seventh century. The earliest part of the church you see standing was was built in the twelfth century, and was built over an earlier monastic site founded by St Tola, a female saint. Very close to the north-west rear of the church is the remains of a round tower that was built possibly in the tenth century. The Romanesque doorway in the south is a must-see. Early medieval church-es had their main entrances in the west of the church, but by the fifteenth century they shifted their position to the south side of the nave. Also if you take a short walk to the east you will find a great example of a High Cross, dating from the twelfth century and rightfully claiming to be one of the finest examples of such carvings in Ireland. It was known as the cross of Manawla or Banola, who was proba-bly Tola the aforementioned female saint, whose crozier is now held in the Royal Irish Academy.

HIGH CROSS REAR SIDE

HIGH CROSS FRONTAL

In this region the early monks settled and often built round towers–across Ireland to this day these enigmatic buildings are still being discovered beneath scrub and vegetation. I will mention the topic again in our next stop. If you exit the field by the gate or stile beyond the cross, you can walk a short distance before turning left down an old driveway to visit a fine specimen of a fifteenth century castle, or Gaelic tower house, belonging to the O'Dea clan. There is an official archaeological walk from the castle that takes in around 25 sites on a 4km walk, including a famine soup kitchen and a rath or medieval ring fort.

RESUME WHEN READY

Return to where you parked your vehicle and continue down the road. Take the second turning on the left and soon you will arrive at a dead end where you can park on front of Rath Church.

POINT C: LOUGH RAHA /RATH BLATHMAIC 52.919564, -9.085549

2.5 km

LAKE RAHA

This is another extremely peaceful spot associated with an early saint. Look to your left and see the lake in the distance–this is Lough Raha, legendary home to a monstrous phantom badger that used to terrorize the local residents. St MacCreehy, who is also associated with chasing a dragon into Liscannor Bay to the west, used his magical powers here to tame the Brock Shee, or fairy badger. He trapped it in a local cave and then threw it in chains into Lake Raha. It is said that every seven years the badger rises again to haunt the people. This tale hints at extraordinary forces in the landscape round here. In my book *Spirit of the Burren* I explain how dragons are symbols of strong invisible forces in the Earth. Wherever there are myths associated with the wandering McCreehy I take note as his role seemed to straddle pagan and early Christian times. He definitely was sensitive to earth energies and was drawn to places that were sacred in pre-Christian times. He is featured on the Lahinch Trail 2 at Liscannor where about a hundred years ago a dragon-like beast was displayed on his gravestone, according to Westropp the historian. The stone is unfortunately no longer there, and few know about St McCreehy these days.

Notice how Rath Church overlooks the lake–this landscape presents a classical "geomantic" scenario in which a tower, or fort (which is the meaning of 'rath') is placed beside a pool of water. The combination of tower and water makes for a harmonious flow of energy. There *was* a round tower close to this church – the local farmer told me he can remember in his childhood how his father would recycle some of its stones. He mentioned a low lying field beside the church where he reckoned it once stood–this seems an odd place to build a tower. In other old annals there is mention of two round towers located on the ridge lying behind the church, again overlooking the lake. Legend has it that one of the round towers was taken by St Tola to the church you have just seen at Dysart. To me this hints at a telluric connection between both sites. The early Christian monks seemed aware of invisible forces in the land. Their orchestrated construction of round towers utilized the silica within the limestone as a semi-conductor. The towers facilitated a store of subtle forms of solar energies that were converted into beneficial forces that were then dispersed over the hinterland, rendering lands more fertile. Entomologist Professor Callahan has done the foremost research into the subtle energies of round towers.

Rath church was founded in the seventh century by St Blathmaic, whose fine crozier and bell are now in the safekeeping of the Irish Arts Academy. The church displays rather an unusual feature known as a sheelagh-na-gig–such crude figures of females displaying their genitalia were carved in stone on old churches throughout Ireland. It could be said that the 'sheela-na-gigs' are to Ireland what the 'green men' are to the UK! No one really knows their original purpose. It may be to ward off evil spirits or it may be to mark a place that was associated with a more ancient religion where the divine feminine was honoured in nature. Of course it could be a bit of both!

Although sheelagh-na-gigs usually looked out over the lintel as in one church we shall see soon, this one is placed inverted inside the left hand side of the south door. It may have been moved when repairing the wall. The church and entire setting exudes a wonderfully peaceful feeling–there is at least one subterranean burial chamber here.

RESUME WHEN READY

Return up the cul de sac and turn right – when you get to the first T junction after about a kilometre turn left, and then very shortly turn right at the next junction onto the main road where you continue to Corofin. There is an unusual Egyptian style stone cross known as the Tau Cross on display in a small heritage museum in the village. It is manned by volunteer staff so check the opening hours *by taking the Gort road to the right in the centre of the village–just past the church on your right is a genealogy/ information centre run by the National Parks and Wildlife Services.* Ask in there if the heritage museum is open. *It is situated just further up on the left inside a small converted church.* If it is closed, further on this trail you can see a replica of the Tau cross, close to its original site.

POINT D: COROFIN HERITAGE MUSEUM 52.944914, -9.063088 4.1 km

RESUME WHEN READY

Now return to the main street and turn right. You may notice on the left hand side a dark orange building protruding onto the street. This is Bofey Quinns pub–the publican is a fisherman and great chef among other things so it it is worth at least trying his chowder! On Wednesday and Saturday evenings the locals play live traditional music there.

Follow the road out of the village and at the junction take the right hand turn for Lisdoonvarna. After about three kilometres you will see an old church on the hill. It stands above a side road marked L5260. You can park a little beyond it on the right hand side in a large lay-by. **Be careful parking as traffic can be quite fast, and the bends restrict visibility.**

POINT E: KILNABOY CHURCH 52.973248, -9.085404   3.5 km

There was an early monastery here dedicated to St Innerwee—or 'St Inghean Baoith' in Irish. This church too sports the stumpy remains of a round tower and a sheela na gig!

The gable end that faces the road has a strange-shaped cross in it – this is the Cross of Lorraine which also features on a boundary stone to old Templar lands I know in Scotland. It seems to be a protective symbol. The cross was carried by Joan of Arc into battle, and it had been used in the Crusades too. Delving into the more esoteric side of history, it could denote that whoever resided at the time the church was built here was connected to a rich inner tradition held within Christianity, which later was lost with the over-Romanization of Christianity. The enigmatic cross is commonly believed to be a sign that the Roman Church kept a portion of the cross Jesus carried.

RESUME WHEN READY

Drive on for about two kilometres. As you reach the top of the hill there is a lay-by on the left that you can pull into and park– there is metal farm gate in the hedge to recognise it by. Carefully walk further on keeping close to the hedge, and around the bend on the same side is a small opening that leads into a fine replica of the Tau cross kept in the museum.

PHOTO ENNIS 6: TAU CROSS REPLICA

The original cross was found near here. It could have been a boundary marker for the female saint's parish. It also could have marked an important pilgrim route to Kilfenora Cathedral nearby. The double-headed symbol is very rare, and in the Christian esoteric tradition reflects knowledge of the deep spiritual meanings stemming from ancient Hebrew letters.

In the cathedral the high crosses gathered in from the nearby fields display some interesting carvings. One of the carvings depicts a cleric carrying a T-shaped crozier in a similar style to the Tau cross, only without the heads either end. A little further on the road rises alongside Roughan Hill, a hill that has been partly excavated to reveal extensive early metal workings. There is a rock on the hill where St Innerwee sat and it is supposed to cure backaches. Perhaps you have been driving too long you might want to sit on it: unfortunately it is on private land!

RESUME WHEN READY.

Return towards Kilnaboy by turning right out of the lay-by. As you go downhill, take the first road on the left labelled L5096– just past a bungalow with three dormer (attic) windows facing the road. This is a very narrow winding road that takes you up onto Roughan Hill which is riddled with archaeological monuments and testifies to a dense population dwelling here in ancient times. After the first kilometre or so the road makes a sharp hair pin bend. When it straightens out again and the vista widens beyond the hazel scrub, there is a fine example of a wedge tomb on the left in the field–you may stop on the roadside. There is a distinct boulder on the right hand side in the field and the large tomb lies opposite on your left.

WEDGE TOMB AT PARKNABINNIA AT DUSK

This hill has many examples of prehistoric activity from the late Neolithic to early Bronze Age (3000-4000 BC). For instance, Carleton Jones excavated an unusual U-shaped court tomb that is 400 metres further west of this tomb. While a classic court tomb has a U shaped courtyard on front of a rectangular cairn, the one here has a narrow unroofed entrance passage (instead of a courtyard) and a U shaped cairn, or burial area. Within Ireland this rare variety of court chamber, is only found in the southern Burren, where there are only four of them!

RESUME WHEN READY.

Now drive on up the hill, and when the road levels out continue until you see a bungalow on the right with a white PVC porch. It is set at an angle to the road. You can park in the open area before it. From here a footpath runs to the right of the bungalow. To access the path, pass through the turnstile, and view the information board on the large fort you are about to visit. This walk is highly recommended. It is a little steep towards the end. It takes you through some pleasant limestone country before it climbs a short distance through the hazel scrub onto a plateau–as you continue on the path a breathtaking view of a large fortification will unfold.. Follow the path towards the fort pitched on the edge of a deep limestone ravine.

POINT H: CAHERCOMMAUN FORT/GLASGEIVNAGH 53.011169, -9.082016   2.5 km

There are about 1500 Iron Age forts in the Burren. Otherwise known as cashels or cahers, forts such as Cahercommaun here were surely of great local significance. It is splendidly perched on the edge of an inland cliff. It is reminiscent of Dun Aengus on Inis Mor's coastal cliffs, as it's enclosed by three concentric drystone walls. It is the inner enclosure that reveals signs of habitation from the fifth century AD until the ninth century, when the present fort was constructed. Signs of iron working, wool shearing and spinning, and even Viking arrowheads have been found upon excavation. There are places in the Burren that indicate occasional inland penetration by the Viking invaders. In the souterrains, jewellery has been found including an enamel piece and a fine silver brooch. If you turn right before the site and walk parallel to the cliffs inland, you enter the hill of Glasgavnagh, where a mythical cow named Glasha grazed. Lon mac Liomtha, a wizard smith, had stolen this grey-green cow from Spain, and she supplied an never-ending flow of milk. Where she lay resting each night on Slieve na Glasha, the grass never grew to this day. Slieve na Glasha is the local hill overlooking a long escarpment. Glasha's milk was everlasting until a cunning local woman tricked Lon by milking her over a sieve. Then her milk ran through, and swiftly turned into seven streams tumbling over the escarpment. In the growing season it's very hard to see the Seven Streams of Glasha from below, as hazel scrub completely camouflages them. Glasha's owner Lon, the fairy smith, had only one leg that grew from the centre of his chest. With this he bounded all over Ireland until he met his fate with Finn Mac Cumhail of the incoming new race, who eventually over-ran him. You can imagine Lon bounding across this boundless plateau! There are many interesting features to see, including a dolmen built into a stone wall. When you have explored enough, return to your car by finding the path that leads down from the fort area.

RESUME WHEN READY

Continue on the same road for .7km and park on the tiny green verge you see on the right towards the bottom of the hill. Before you park you may spot on the right the cliffs of Cahercommaun looming above the forest, and then when you park you can look through gaps in the undergrowth across at the fort you have just visited. You are surrounded by hazel forest here, and if you walk a few paces on you may see a gap in the wall on the left. This leads onto a path that veers to the left in the forest clearing. Lower yourselves off the wall onto the forest floor and follow the footpath for about ten minutes. When you see the low cliffs on your left, either walk along the base of these following a natural path or continue on a little more until you see the cave entrance in the cliffs. This cave is now sealed with a gate, but it is where there was a significant discovery of bones found in a cairn inside the cave, revealing upon analysis that a significantly high proportion of local people are descended from those who were buried in a ritual manner here four thousand years or more ago! The woods are very beautiful to walk through slowly. Do not pick any wild flowers please, or leave any litter.

Return to your car and continue on, passing a turning to the right after a few kilometres. You will pass a ruin of a castle on the right past the turning. Turn right at the main junction onto a wider road, to drive alongside one of the Burren's largest turloughs or disappearing lakes. During dry periods the base of the lake is exposed. Plants growing here have to adapt to long periods of drowning. Cassidy's pub in Carron overlooks the turlough on the right, and is a pleasant place to stop if open. *Go through the village, passing the turning to the right you will be taking later—it is signposted to the Burren Perfumery. A short way beyond the village take a small turning to the right, signposted to Temple Cronan. Go down there to the end and park near the farm walls. Walk in to the right along a track and then over a stile—cross the field diagonally to the right along a slight path and cross another stile. This takes you into a hidden hollow where there is a small church. As you set off across the field you will only be able to see its gable ends rising from the dip in the land.*

POINT I: ST CRONAN'S CARRON 53.04885, -9.064091   5.2 km

This is a fine example of an early Christian church with typical small windows. The simple cell church is decorated with heads of animals and humans in the Romanesque style. Like many such churches it roughly measures 13 feet by 21 feet. This is a Golden Mean ratio rectangle, which in mathematical terms sets the breadth and length in the proportion of 1 by 1. 618 respectively. This ratio is prevalent in many life forms and in classical times was liberally applied in architecture to create harmony. There are some interesting tomb shrines outside the church that might have housed relics of St Cronan who founded a monastery here—the monastic buildings have disappeared but there are traces visible under the grass.

ST CRONAN'S RELIQUARY AND CHURCH

One of the tomb shrines is over the wall beyond the east gable of the church. There are also monastic field systems and boundary walls nearby. Walk over the stile south of the church and follow the path at the base of some cliffs, and you come to another stile that leads into a small holy well at the foot of a cliff. There is an interesting mound beside it that looks like an ancient cairn, though some local guides seem to ignore it. There is a standing stone on the top of this mound. This arrangement of standing stone by holy water was common in earlier Christian times. Many places were sabotaged upon order of the Catholic church in more recent times. This broke the connection with earlier traditions and also disempowered the land on an energetic level. So Temple Cronan is a special place that deserves our respect and nurturing.

STANDING STONE BY ST CRONAN'S WELL

RESUME WHEN READY

Now drive back to the main road and head left back into the village. Take the first turning to the left and travel on for about three kilometres until you reach a viewpoint offering marvellous views over the Eastern Burren hills. This overlooks Fahee North.

POINT J: VIEWPOINT, FAHEE 53.047612, -9.034935   5 km

The display boards explain about the geology and topology of the area.

RESUME WHEN READY.

Continue on the road and go through the small village of Glencolumkille and take the first turning on the right. It is less than two kilometres on from Fahee. Travel on this road for a less than four kilometres and look out for a large farmhouse set up a long driveway with gates, on the right hand side.

POINT K: FR. TED'S HOUSE 53.017055, -9.022377   5.8 km

Welcome to Fr. Ted's house! This was featured at the start of each TV Father Ted programme in a popular comedy series shown around the world. Regrettably the actor died in the prime of his life. If you book in advance you can enjoy tea and cakes here.

FATHER TED'S HOUSE

RESUME WHEN READY

Carry on the same road and after six kilometres you reach the Corofin road that runs past Kilnaboy Church seen on the right, towering over the junction. Turn left towards Corofin. In the village continue straight through, going over the River Fergus bridge, and carry on straight towards Ennis once more.

Ennis 22.9km

End of Ennis Trail